GROWING UP HARD IN HARLAN COUNTY

GROWING UP HARD IN HARLAN COUNTY

G.C. Jones

With a Foreword by
Cratis Williams

THE UNIVERSITY PRESS
OF KENTUCKY

Title page and chapter opening page illustrations
are from *At Home in the Hills: Glimpses of
Harlan County, Kentucky*, by John A. Spelman III.
Courtesy of Pine Mountain Settlement School.

Copyright © 1985 by The University Press of Kentucky

Scholarly publisher for the Commonwealth,
serving Bellarmine College, Berea College, Centre
College of Kentucky, Eastern Kentucky University,
The Filson Club, Georgetown College, Kentucky
Historical Society, Kentucky State University,
Morehead State University, Murray State University,
Northern Kentucky University, Transylvania University,
University of Kentucky, University of Louisville,
and Western Kentucky University.

Editorial and Sales Offices: Lexington, Kentucky 40506-0024

Library of Congress Cataloging in Publication Data
Jones, G. C. (Green C.), 1913-

Growing up hard in Harlan County.

1. Jones, G. C. (Green C.), 1913-   . 2. United
Mine Workers of America—History. 3. Coal-miners—
Kentucky—Harlan County—Biography. 4. Trade-unions—
Kentucky—Harlan County—Organizing—History. 5. Harlan
County (Ky.)—Biography. 6. Harlan County (Ky.)—Economic
conditions. 7. Harlan County (Ky.)—Social life and
customs. I. Title.
HD6509.J66A34   1985   331.88'122334'0924 [B]   84-7458
ISBN 0-8131-1521-3

FOR MAE
my first and only love

FOREWORD

MOST ATTEMPTS at autobiography by native Appalachian folk, even retired schoolteachers with college degrees, fail to arouse reader interest. The writer, too often doubting the value of his own story, seeks protection in moral posturing and treats the reader to platitudes and commonplaces, or dilutes the account with generous servings of imitative "fine writing" that alienate the reader after a few pages. Rarely does one come upon a native writer with both a talent for telling a story and a genius for investing it with power. G.C. Jones is such a writer. *Growing Up Hard in Harlan County*, simply told but with subtlety and strength, despite its candor, is a celebration of Appalachian oral tradition.

Jones—whose life spans the age of change in Harlan County, from the 1920s, when it was a thinly settled agrarian region in which styles of living had changed but little since settlement days, through the bloody coal wars of the 1930s, to the collapse of the coal industry in the 1950s—has given us, in the powerful and refreshing idiom of the people, a social and economic report as well as a folkloric history of life there.

Social historians have documented what life was like in Harlan County when families lived at a comfortable subsistence level on mountain farms, made and sold moonshine whiskey, hunted and trapped for pelts, and gathered walnuts and herbs to transport in high-sided dragsleds over roads that lay in the beds of streams to stores at crossroads villages or to the muddy little town of Harlan itself to barter for cloth, shoes, salt, and hardware, and enough cash in hand to pay their taxes. The rapid growth of the coal industry, with its record of exciting booms and wrenching busts, attendant violence in the struggle of miners to unionize, and corruption of public officials by operators, has been reported. The agonies of the Great Depression and the poverty left in the wake of the coal industry's collapse, are subjects of common knowledge. G.C. Jones's straightforward, honest, and delightfully refreshing account of his experiencing this history, participating in the struggle, enjoying the excitement of change, and suffering through the violence and bloodshed, betrayal and corruption, brings the reader immediately into the midst of a shocking reality.

Growing Up Hard in Harlan County moves with the speed of a cliff-hanger novel, but the narrative style is that of the teller of folktales. While Jones was a youngster driving his own team of "big blacks" across Pine Mountain, he and fellow teamsters swapped stories around campfires at night. It was here that he mastered the craft of storytelling, a craft that he perfected as a sailor in World War II, as a hobo, and as a genial host. His is an unselfconscious narrator. His keen mind, accurate memory, understanding, compassion, and sensitivity to his surroundings are brought together as one in his powerful story of pioneer self-reliance, courage, and triumph over terrifying adversity.

The most refreshing aspects of his book are Jones's expansiveness of style without the irrelevancies that expansiveness invites, and his amplitude of language. He is a master of his medium. His account moves at a colloquial level and as familiarly as a fireside chat. Jones reports the "grub" that mountain people eat—corn pone, shucky beans, taters, sorghums, and dried apple stack cake. A glossary of the vocabulary of teamsters, one of our lost occupations, may be gathered from his account of his early life. He spins a tale in a living dialect so easily and charmingly that we marvel at the literary power of that dialect.

Like his friend JoJo, Jones can "make a hand" at anything he wants to do. Rejected, driven out of his family, betrayed and buffeted by circumstances, he never once sinks into self-pity. He tells us that he is a "woods colt," but that knowledge does not damage his sense of worth, for in Appalachia one proves himself with his own individuality, ability, and shrewdness. Jones has the primal strength of the Appalachian pioneer. He has translated that strength inimitably into this candid autobiography, a first-hand account of what life was like in Harlan County during the most convulsive period in the history of Appalachia.

CRATIS WILLIAMS

PREFACE

BEFORE I get started on this writing, I'd like to tell a little about myself. I was the fifth child in a family of eight. My bringing up was under hard and strict parents. When they spoke to any one of us kids, we were quick to do their bidding.

My family were good livers. We raised nearly everything we ate, and plenty of grain and fodder for our stock. A good size stream flowed near the barn. This is where we penned our butchering animals. We raised a lot of extra calves, hogs, chickens, ducks, and many many other things to take to the town of Harlan to offer for sale or to trade. The town people were eager to get our country-fresh foods. Some people called us peddlers.

Now, Harlan was a small but fast growing coal mining town. You'll read a lot more about it farther in this writing. This was a beautiful country, mostly large mountains, narrow valleys, and streams filled with fish. The mountains held plenty of game—deer, bear, wild hogs, panther, bobcats. Just about any kind of game you wanted, it was there for your taking.

All of this was to change in a few short years. Harlan County, Kentucky, has had several bloodbaths since progress moved in. I know, and I am going to write all I know about it.

I'm not going to use the real names of some of the people I write about because their kin might become embarrassed knowing they made their livelihood from moonshine whiskey. But all the other names are of real people.

I didn't get very much schooling, but I aim to do the best I can to tell you of the experiences I've got stored up in me.

GROWING UP HARD IN HARLAN COUNTY

ONE

AS FAR BACK as I can remember I always had a lot of chores to be responsible for, such as getting the milk cows out of the mountains to the barn, slopping hogs, weeding the garden. It seems like I could go on for days just sitting here reminiscing about the early years of my childhood.

I come from a big family, four brothers and four sisters. Artie, the first born, was followed by Narciss, then Sophia, then Jim, and then myself, Green. Then came William, Dave, and my youngest sister, Cecil. Another baby died at one month's age.

Artie had flaming red hair, just like mine. She was nine years older than me. There was so much house work for her to do she couldn't enjoy herself like the younger kids. Artie had to help Mom prepare canned foods for the cold winter. They canned beans and corn.

They pickled beans and corn, too. You string and snap the beans and cut the corn off the cob whole kernel, then cram pack them well mixed into fifty-gallon wood barrels, cover with hog curing salt, put this in a non-freezing place, and let it pickle. It sure is good eating with corn pone, side pork, buttermilk, and a big onion. My mouth drools when I think of them cold winter days, the aroma coming from the kitchen and going all through the house.

Now, where I grew up was a mountain country in Harlan County, Kentucky. The valleys were very narrow, most of them not being wide enough for a road and the creek. You had to use the creek bed for a road. Most every family used a horse or mule hooked to a high runner sled to traverse their mountain grown produce to the town of Harlan to trade it for store commodities. It was seldom heard of, someone selling their produce for cash. They would trade for salt, sugar, soda, shoes, a few bags of flour, sometimes a bag of horehound candy for the kids to lick on.

Around Christmas time a large load of winter farm produce such as furs, cowhides, black walnuts, and a few jugs of real good corn liquor would be taken to Harlan or to one of the nearby coal camps. These items would be sold or traded for the nicer things, such as a crank phonograph, banjo or guitar strings, harmonicas, and a few bolts of pretty dress cloth for the girls. All this made a happy Christmas.

I was about six years old when I recall the first load of winter materials to be traded for Christmas goodies. Everyone in the family got some kind of gift or toy. For me, I got my first pair of long-johns, about four sizes too large. I thought they were the greatest thing anyone could own, for the winters on these mountains could be mighty cold.

My folks didn't go in for all the gee-jaws of home furnishings. We had feather bed ticks or corn shuck ticks for mattresses and big thick bed quilts. Nearly all the furniture was hand-made. Dad boasted about his art for building anything for the home except the cooking stove.

When all the day's work was done and everyone was preparing for bed, it was my job to drag the fire, let the old barn cat in, put the kindling wood by the fireplace, and blow out the oil lamps. Then I'd dash for the ladder to the attic and crawl into bed.

My older brother Jim did the heavier work. Jim, who was always helping Dad with work stock, drove a team of horses or big Missouri mules, hauling supplies from wholesale freight depots across Pine Mountain, on down Straight Creek, and across Kentucky Ridge to families and little country stores that had settled there. The wagons would be loaded with nearly everything, like farm tools, harnesses, coal oil, sugar, seeds, barb-wire, canning jars, dress cloth, and nails.

Since the railroad came to Harlan, the people over these mountains started ordering more up-to-date farm machinery, such as hillside turning plows, hay rakes, and mowing machines, and some ordered scratch plows. They never heard of these things before the boom started moving in Harlan and money began flowing over the mountains for their farm produce and moonshine. Dad, seeing the demand growing for hauling over the mountains, started buying and trading for big Morgan and Percheron horses. He bought the biggest mules he could find. The wagons were three-inch Conestoga; they could carry a five-ton load. But a single span couldn't pull a load this heavy over the mountain. Nearly always he had to use two spans.

It was nine miles from the foot of Pine Mountain to the top. The single spans would be doubled. That is, one wagon would remain at the foot of the mountain and the driver would raise his span to double-team the wagon ahead. This method was used until all the wagons topped the mountain. Sometimes it would be into the night before all the wagons made the top.

Each wagon driver carried his own provisions—meal, flour, water, coffee pot, spider, skillet, sidemeat, feed for his stock, ground sheet, and an old quilt. On top of these mountains the nights sure got cold. After the stock had been rubbed down, watered, and fed, the aroma of frying side pork and hoe-johnny bread and strong black coffee smelled good. Some good mother or wife would roll up a jar of home canned peaches or apples to top off a good mountain supper.

After supper was over everybody gathered around the main campfire, swapping woman tales, stories about hog raising or breeding cattle, swapping pocket knives, and different ways to make moonshine. This would go long into the night. After a while some of the men would ease away to their wagons and crawl into their snoogins. Someone would bring out his old french harp. You just ain't never heard more beautiful music than these old mountain boys could make with their harps.

When you thought everyone was sacked in, someone who missed his girlfriend or his wife would drift away to the edge of camp and break out with some of the lonesomest love songs you ever heard, while you were lying there trying to go to sleep, with every muscle aching from all the work it took to gain the top of the mountain.

The wagon road was more of a trail than a road. Sometimes after hard rains it would take hours to carry rocks, poles, logs, and fill-in dirt to these washed-out places. It was a man and beast killing road. Some of the rises were so steep that two-span and three-span teams could move a wagon not over five feet at a pull.

Dad put me to choking on my brother's wagon, him being the youngest driver on the wagons. I was nine and Jim was twelve. He could handle a team of horses with the best of care. He was not very big but he was strong.

After a pull, with me behind with my scotch block set, and the check line secured at the foot rest line stick, Jim would get hold of the spokes of a front wheel and call on the lead horse. The big bay Morgan would begin moving his feet to get good footing. He and the other three would really get down to work. Jim would pull on the spokes, trace chains would ring, leather collars would screech, and the wagon would move a short distance. With my scotch block in my hands I would place it at the right time. The block was made of oak, a foot and a half long and ten inches thick. The wagon would stop, with the horses' flanks heaving, sweat dripping off them and their muscles trembling. This was a fine team of horses.

Dad always gave the best of care to his stock. It was a must to rub down each animal, check all their feet for loose shoes and hoof cracks, rub their shoulders good, and check for any kind of strained muscle or sore mouth from bit strain. We checked over the entire wagon for loose bolts. Each wheel had iron tires, so we used real stiff axle grease on each axle spinnel. I was very observant in all this care. It was my aim to become one of the famed drivers.

The next two years I got in a lot of experience. If a driver for some reason could not show up, I was to take his place. The owner of the team would make arrangements with Dad for me to drive.

By the time I was twelve years old I was driving for an old man. I'll call him Bill Ford, though that wasn't his real name. He owned several wagons and eighteen of the finest Morgan and Percheron horses that ever came to these hills. He also owned a span of big, coal black mules. They looked like twins, each weighing about 1,600 pounds, and five years old. Very few drivers liked to drive mules when they could sit in the seat behind a span of prancing Morgans. Lots of days these mules stayed in the barn.

One cold chilly morning before dawn I was at the barn, going over my harness and getting ready for a large load of staple food to be hauled over Pine Mountain. The wholesale, H.T. Hackney Company, was sending ten wagons on this trip. Mr. Ford was sending me and four more of his wagons. My Dad was taking two wagons, with my brother Jim driving one of them. We were to have our teams and wagons at the wholesale loading dock at seven o'clock. I always tried to be early on the job.

I got my two Morgans and led them to the harness shed. As I opened the door to the shed two big Walker hounds ran out. They had been put in the shed the night before to breed. They darted among my horses. One of the horses, Old Bob, reared and came down flailing his forefeet. One of his legs hit a protruding log, which resulted in a leg lame.

I wrapped Old Bob's leg with strips of a feed sack. As I was quieting the horses, Mr. Ford came around the corner of the barn. I called to him as he came up. One look from Mr. Ford at the injured horse showed me the love he had for his stock. He came over to my side, holding the lantern so it would shine on the horse's wounded leg. After a close look, he turned to me with a shocked look on his face and said, "It feels like he's got a cracked bone at the base of the fetlock. He also has a split hoof."

Now you'd think that my job with Mr. Ford would be over, but not so. He raised up, hung the lantern on a peg, placed his hand on my shoulder, and said, "Well, son, it 'pears like your Morgans are not going to make this trip. It will be quite a while before he heals."

I just stood there for a moment, although it seemed like hours, with a sickening feeling running through me. I knew this would be the end of my driving career with Mr. Ford for this season. He must have sensed my feelings. After I led the other horse over to the barn, I came back to the shed to see about moving Old Bob to the barn. As I approached, Mr. Ford was trying to get the horse from under the shed canopy. This Morgan was a big horse. We got him turned around, but he could not put any weight on the injured leg.

As I stood there, shaking all over, I wanted to do something to help. Mr. Ford told me to carry a bundle of hay from the barn and fix up the feed box over near the widest part of the sheltered shed. After doing all this, we began to rummage through the shed for something to sling the horse off the ground. When Mr. Ford put up a building, he made it strong and from the best of logs. Overhead, where the horse was to be slung, were rafters with eight-inch by ten-inch logs. The ceiling was about ten feet high.

Now, most of the mountain people don't have very much book learning or flatland people's ways of tackling a job that requires skill. We just look at the situation right in the eye and make up our mind of what to do with the problem ahead.

It was now getting good daylight. We carried all the hoisting to where we were to raise the horse. There had been a derailed train near Harlan about two months before. Mr. Ford got the job clearing all the wreck. A lot of the wreckage was very hard to handle, so he had bought three or four big heavy chain blocks and had these hung up in the harness shed. We managed to hang these chain blocks to the overhead logs and got some discarded sawmill belting for padding. We placed the belting under the horse and secured each end to a chain block.

Now, Old Bob was very gentle. He seemed to know we were trying to do something for him. Mr. Ford got hold of the pull chain on one side and I got on the other. We started pulling about the same time and very, very gently we raised the horse's front feet about four inches off the ground.

I rigged a water box for Old Bob, put some corn and oats in his feed box. He seemed like he was well contented. We left him like this and walked over to the barn. As we came up to the door, Mr. Ford turned to me and said, "I sure need to have your wagon on this haul." He asked me if I could handle the team of big mules on this trip. I said I could if I could have a good scotcher up the mountain.

By now all the other drivers were at the barn preparing their teams for the trip to the wholesale to load their wagons. They were all curious as to what had happened to my Morgan. We told them as we went on our way, getting the team of big black mules hitched to my wagon.

It was about five miles from Mr. Ford's to the wholesale. I was the first to start off. These mules had not been worked any for near a month. We harnessed them with newly made gear, brass hames, all shiny, and new bridle tassels and hip tassels. The other drivers were awfully proud of the big clumsy Morgans. But if their expressions were called proudness, I can't think of a word that would describe my feelings as I sat high on my seat and drove the prancingest team of black mules that ever came to these mountains.

After getting all the wagons loaded and the tarps tied down, we took off for the foot of Pine Mountain. My position was number five, just ahead of my brother Jim. The wagon ahead was driven by a small colored man by the name of Jesse Renfro. His team was owned by Uncle Hamp Huff. Uncle Hamp (no kin to me) had the only leather and harness shop within fifty to seventy-five miles, so with all the boom of harness work to do he could well afford to own some of the best stock and the shiniest harness.

As we came to the base of Pine Mountain we circled our wagons, cared for the stock, fixed a good supper of fried corn pone, taters, sidemeat, plenty of good springhouse-cooled sweet milk, and buttermilk. We got the milk from the wife of the one-time sheriff of Harlan, Peg Leg Will Roark. She gave us the buttermilk and charged us ten cents a gallon for the sweet milk. I can remember how creamy it was. This sure was a good camp supper.

We had a huge fire in the center of our circle. When it was settling into darkness, Will Roark and two of his sons and his wife came to the edge of the camp and called out to ask if they could come in. We welcomed them to enter. Here they came, him waddling along with a fiddle in his hand, and his two sons, one with a banjo, the other with nothing but one of the mellowest voices you ever heard. Mrs. Roark held in her hand some old-time mountain ballads.

As they gathered around the fire everyone rose up to greet them. Mrs. Roark asked if we would like to hear some old-time singing with music. We all welcomed it.

Mr. Roark twanged his fiddle strings to catch the tone he wanted to play. He then stroked his bow over the strings. His wife stepped up near him and said, "I would like to sing with my son one of all mountain people's favorites, 'Give Me That Old Time Religion.' " After the first verse, everyone started to clap and joined in with the singing. We sure enjoyed their company till about ten o'clock. Then, bidding everyone good-night, we all turned to our snoogins for a good restful sleep.

Around four o'clock the next morning everyone was up, feeding and caring for their stock. I got my big black mules and led them down to the creek and let them drink all they wanted, then took them back to camp. I gave them their grain, brushed them down good, then went to Dad's wagon for a bite to eat. He had a bag of Mom's big biscuits all heated up, and good thick sorghums and black coffee.

By six o'clock all the teams were hitched and ready to take to the mountain. I got to keep my position. A lot of the men came around, giving me advice on how to handle my mules. Sometimes mules can get awful stubborn, but these were gentle and good natured.

So with all my friends' advice we started up the mountain. My scotcher was a very close friend of mine. His name was JoJo Walters, short for Joseph. He was more or less a town boy. Of course, Harlan wasn't much of a town at that time. Harlan had no paved streets or bridges, but yet it was our town, and he grew up there. It was told around that he would steal anything he could carry off, but that's not so. I have spent many days with JoJo and I always found him to be trusted. That's why I got him to work on my wagon.

As we neared the first hard climb all the wagons came to rest for about twenty or thirty minutes. I got my water pail and gave each mule about one gallon of water. I knew these mules were not broken to mountain work, so I was giving them extra close attention. I pushed my hand under their collar pad and let in cool air to their sweaty shoulders and checked their head gear and bits. If a shoe came loose I would get my hammer and clinching iron and tighten the nails.

We got started after a short rest. The next seven and a half miles to the top were steep and rough. JoJo was doing a fine job scotching. After placing the large oak block at the base of a hind wheel, he would scramble for a big rock to put at the other wheel. I would let the blacks slack off their traces and let them wind for about a minute and a half. Then we would go for another short pull. JoJo seemed like he was enjoying his job.

Some of the heavier wagons had to double-team over some of the worst stretches. When we came to the big flat area nearly halfway up the mountain we unhitched our teams, rubbed them down good, and gave them about a gallon of water and a lick of salt and a small amount of hay.

While our stock was munching hay, each man brought out his lunch basket. Jesse Renfro was no larger than me, but he had a basket with enough food in it to feed a dozen men. He had fried chicken and biscuits with real cow butter and homemade wild grape jelly between each one. On top of it he had two big molassie stack cakes; the layers were put together with old-time dried apples with plenty of sweetened spice.

Everybody got something from his basket and some of the men were teasing Jesse about how good his food was. Some of them had never eaten a bite of Negro cooking. Jesse told us his boss's wife, Aunt Can Huff, brought the basket to him as he climbed into the wagon. She told him to enjoy it with all the other men on the drive. He made a lot of white friends, as this was his first trip on a wagon train. He made a lot more trips in years to come.

After we put our grubs back in our larder, we hitched our teams and started the rest of the climb to the top. About an hour after we started the second wagon in front of me stalled. The driver, a big raw-boned man of about thirty years of age, was thrashing his horses with a big nine-plait black snake whip and cursing them like a demon. This team belonged to Mr. Ford.

JoJo choked my wagon good and I walked ahead to the stalled team. I asked the driver to stop beating his horses. He told me to mind my own damn business or he would give me a few cracks with his black snake whip. That sorta shook me up. Never before had I been talked to like that.

The two drivers up front came walking down to the stalled wagon. There I stood, about as scared as I ever was in my life, not knowing hardly what to do or say. Then JoJo and this man's scotcher came from behind the wagon. Our new friend Jesse and his scotcher appeared also. JoJo climbed the bank above this big driver, grabbing a big rock in each hand, looked down to the driver, and told him, "Go ahead and crack him with your whip. It will be the last damn crack you will make!"

The man threw his whip to the ground, mumbled a few words, then climbed up in the wagon and got his personal gear from the foot locker. As he got to the ground, he turned to me and said, "You red-headed bastard, I'll find you when you're grown to a man, then I'll beat the hell out of you!"

He started toward me with his hand drawn back to hit me. JoJo cut loose with a rock about as big as a pint jar, hitting him on the left side of his jaw. He fell like an ox.

The other drivers came rushing up to see what happened. Dad and my brother Jim came to me and wanted to know what happened. I explained in a shaky voice. About that time Jesse dashed his hat full of water in the injured man's face. You could tell his jaw was broken by the way his mouth stayed gaped open. Dad went over and knelt beside him and asked if he could make it back to Harlan. He nodded his head that he could. Dad then told him to get out and to catch the first thing to get out of that part of the country. If he didn't, a broken jaw would be small at their next meeting.

Someone came over with a long strip of cloth and offered to tie his jaw up. He let them do it, then picked up his roll and took off for Harlan.

There we were with a team and no driver. Mr. Ford's boss driver, Dave Good, was bringing up the tail of the drive. As the injured driver met him, he started trying to go through motions to tell what had happened. He couldn't make his boss understand, so Dave left his scotcher with his team and took off up the mountain. We were waiting for him to take charge of the problem. After looking at the horses and seeing the welts and blood all over them, he told us we should have finished the driver off for good.

Now, Dave was a cool-headed man; he could handle about any kind of a job or difficult problem. He first off wanted to know if there was a scotcher that could manage a team. No one said anything. JoJo looked over to me with a big grin. I waited a minute before I said anything, then I offered my suggestion. Dave told me to go ahead. I started by asking him if I could change the stalled horses to the number one wagon. It was the lightest load of them all and was hitched with the largest horses. I offered to let JoJo take charge of the big blacks and I would take the stalled wagon with the largest team. We each would do our own scotching. He thought this was about the only thing to do, but he warned JoJo and me to be awful careful.

Some of the men came around and clapped for JoJo and me and insisted on changing the horses for me. When the change was made I checked the collars, traces, feet, and bridles, leaving a loose check-rein. I told the drivers I was ready.

I went back and showed JoJo as much as I could in the short time we had because it was getting late. We had about two or two and a half miles of hard climbing before we topped the mountain.

I got back up to the stalled wagon as the ones in front started out. I stopped at the rear and called out to the huge Percherons. They snorted and eased ahead. They felt the load behind them. Then, both horses started at the same time and eased the stalled wagon up and over the steep and rough place.

After a few more short pulls I scotched my wagon good and went back down to check on how JoJo was doing with the big blacks. He had gained about three hundred feet and was doing just fine. This being his first real driving, he was eager to learn all he could. He often told me he wanted to someday own his own team and wagon and sign on for trips over these mountains.

JoJo scotched his wagon good and came up to the big blacks, patting and rubbing their trembling legs and talking to them. He felt under each collar pad and rubbed their shoulders good. As I watched him I knew he was going to make a good driver. To become a handler of stock you've got to know how to care for them. Treat them gentle, watch out for any discomfort that might be caused by bad fitting harness or a strained muscle or ligament. You do this and the animal will learn to obey every command you give.

As I stood there watching JoJo check the mules, mostly giving them a short breathing spell, he asked if I thought he was doing it right. I told him no one could do a better job than he was doing. It sure pleased him and he told me he never expected to have a better friend than me, for getting Mr. Good to allow him to take charge of the big blacks. JoJo didn't mention what happened earlier and I didn't either. I told him to be careful and went back up to my team.

The rest of the road to the top was steep but smooth and we made good time. As all the wagons gained the top, we unhitched and took care of our teams. We then built several small fires near our own wagons and brought out our grub boxes. Everyone had a good supper, then cleared up their dirty pans and crawled into their snoogins.

TWO

THE NEXT MORNING, after all the eating and cleaning up our camp, we started in checking our wagons for any kind of damage that might have happened coming up the mountain. Then we hitched up and took our places with the wagons, to head downhill.

I sure was pleased with the way JoJo was handling his team, sitting up high in his seat. He called out to ask if he could move up to the position ahead of me. Dave came over and told him it would be his choice to have any position he wanted, with the way he was handling them big blacks. "You are going to make a real good driver," he said. All the other drivers agreed with him, JoJo was doing a good job.

Now, it was about two miles from where we topped the mountain to where we started down the other side. As each wagon came to where we turned down, Dave and my dad were there to check and make sure all the brake shoes were in good shape and the rear wheel on the left was equipped with a good heavy chain. One end wrapped around the rim and iron tire. The other end was hooked to a ring bolted to the strong rocking bolster that supported the carriage for the wagon bed. This was called rough locking. As the wagon moved ahead the chain would stop the wheel from rolling and the chain part wrapped around the rim would dig into the ground. This caused the horses to have to pull a little even to get the wagon to go downhill.

When we came to the valley at the foot we loosened our rough lock chains and checked the crates, boxes, and cases in our wagons. It sure was rough coming down. The well-packed loads would be shifted around and holes would tear in the sugar sacks. Cases of other stuff turned over. You just about had to unload and then reload.

The wagons were covered with tarps. We took off down the

valley. That is, some of us did. The others went up the valley to scattered homes and little country stores, dropping off whatever they had ordered.

Me and the other three drivers came to the first farm. We pulled into the barn lot, unharnessed our teams, and were letting them drink. Mr. Morgan came from the house, a big two-story house with a trot. A trot is a covered space between the main house and the kitchen and eating room. He called to us to come in to supper.

We cared for the stock after doing the feeding. We walked down to the creek, stripped our shirts off, and with some homemade yellow lye soap we began to scrub all the dirt and sweat from our upper bodies.

Hanging on an old rail fence were a few dry clothes left there for anyone to use. We dried off, then slipped into a clean rolled-up shirt, washed the mud and dirt off our shoes, and then walked up to Mr. Morgan's. He greeted us and welcomed us to come into the kitchen. As the door swung open, I got the aroma of food and my stomach started to put forth hunger pains.

All the Morgans were having supper. The kitchen and eating room was about a thirty-foot square room, with a wide long table over near two big windows. This was not my first time here. Dad and my brother Jim had been here many times.

After dinner Mr. Morgan walked down to the barn with us. We wanted to grease our wagons and groom our stock. After this was taken care of, it was getting dark, and Mr. Morgan suggested we go to bed. He knew we were tired.

Jesse said he would climb up in the barn to sleep, for he didn't think it proper for a black man to sleep in a white man's house. Mr. Morgan told him to suit himself, but to not pay any attention to the noises he would probably hear during the night.

Jesse asked, "What kind of noise?"

Mr. Morgan told him it was probably wind blowing in and around cracks, or maybe a loose board flapping on the roof. He said, "It sure sounds like someone gasping and moaning."

As he was telling this, Jesse's eyes seemed to be popping out of his head. Mr. Morgan continued on, telling Jesse that the sounds might come from just beneath the barn, where the Yankees had killed and burned about fifty Rebels.

Jesse grabbed Mr. Morgan by the arm and asked if he could sleep on the floor in the big house.

The next morning, after eating a good breakfast of country ham, eggs, gravy, and good syrupy fried apples, we uncovered Jesse's wagon and unloaded what goods were labeled for Mr. Morgan.

We then hooked our teams and continued on our way to the Pine Mountain Settlement School, where most of our loads were labeled to. This school was funded by a church group up in New York. The students were mostly from our region of the country. I had seen several of them around Harlan. They were children from the coal mining camps that were springing up all over Harlan County.

As we drove our big wagons up to the warehouse a lot of the students gathered around, watching and asking questions about the other side of the mountain. We joshed around with them as we unloaded, telling them that some big politician had promised to put in paved streets and build two big high schools. Someone from Lexington, Kentucky, was building a three-story, eighty-room hotel over near the depot.

This seemed to please them. They talked to each other about the coming summer, of how they would get jobs and save their money and start a business after they finished school.

After we unloaded everything labeled to the school, an elderly lady came over and asked us to have some lunch. We accepted her offer and ate hungrily. We thanked her for her kindness, then climbed in our wagons and headed for our next stop.

As we traveled further we passed several big farms. Lots of sheep and cattle dotted the cleared mountainside. Farmers were plowing their lowlands for early planting.

This sure is a beautiful country in the early spring. Dogwoods, sarvis, and redbud trees were in full bloom along pathways. Gates and yards were covered with climbing red roses. As we passed close to some homes, we could see large flocks of chickens out scratching for their newly hatched chicks, or big lots with several big black and white sows suckling their pigs. These hogs' bloodline was called Poland China, a good mountain breed.

We pulled into our next farm to unload two hillside turning plows and four sets of heavy harness. This was Mr. Lisenbee's farm. He owned more bottom ground than any farmer on the creek. He also owned a lot of low-lying ridges that were cleared for cattle grazing. Mr. Lisenbee was one of the richest farmers in the entire county.

It was getting sorta late in the evening and Mr. Lisenbee asked us to have a bite of supper with him. We climbed along the pathway up to the house, ducking our heads under the rose bushes, plucking one here and there to form a small bouquet to hand to Mrs. Lisenbee.

Mrs. Lisenbee was a large woman, with a beautiful red complexion and gray hair twisted into a large bun on the top of her head. She welcomed us to her kitchen.

As we entered, Jesse stayed outside. Mrs. Lisenbee stepped out on the porch and told him he was welcomed to sit at her table. He shook his head and told her he didn't think it proper, him being a black man and sitting among such nice white people. She sure stopped him up quick. She got hold of his arm and just about dragged him to the table. As he sat there on the bench, she told him to be at ease and enjoy his supper. After a couple of helpings of all the food before us, he really got down to eating.

We still had about two or three hours of daylight, so we thanked them for our supper and left. As we came out onto the creek road, we decided one wagon could carry what we had in all three, so we pulled Jesse's wagon up alongside of JoJo's and started moving one-hundred-pound sacks of sugar from Jesse's wagon to JoJo's. I did the same with my wagon.

Jesse and I turned and went back up to Mr. Lisenbee's and got permission to leave our two teams there. A stream ran through the middle of the barn lot. Jesse climbed to the loft and threw down fodder and Mr. Lisenbee gave them plenty of corn.

We then went back to where JoJo was waiting. As we came up to him he was going over the blacks, rubbing and patting them. We climbed up in the wagon and JoJo asked me to drive. He said, "I want to check your way of handling the team to the way I do."

We had seven more miles to go. This included going over Kentucky Ridge, which was about three miles up and two miles down to the other side.

The big blacks started off, prancing and slinging their heads and showing off. They knew they were being commanded by a more experienced driver. JoJo sat beside me, up high in the spring seat, and watched every move I made. He started mimicking my commands to the mules.

Jesse, sitting back in the wagon, watching us, wanted to know how I had become such a good handler of stock and wagons. I told him that since the first time I worked for my brother, my aim was to become the best.

We talked on until we came to the foot of Kentucky Ridge. We stopped and checked the wagon wheels and the harness. Then, with Jesse and JoJo both scotching for me, we made it to the top, with plenty of mule power to spare. We then locked a rear wheel and drifted down. When we got to the foot we could see the house and barn we were headed to.

As we pulled up to the barn a big bearded man came from the house. I called to Mr. Anderson (not his real name) who I was and what I had to deliver. I had forty-two hundred-pound sacks of sugar. This pleased him. He told us to care for the mules and come on over to the house.

When we entered the house, Mrs. Anderson was setting us some food on the table. We had already had an earlier supper, but we said nothing about it. Jesse was getting more broke into white folks' hospitality. He sat down and started to fill his plate. Then he stopped all of a sudden and looked up in the lady's eyes and asked if he could say grace and thanks. She nodded her head. He started off by thanking the Lord for such a great world to live in. Then for being able to deliver all our consigned loads to their destinations. He also asked the Lord to look out for the care of the man JoJo hit with the rock, and to forgive JoJo for hitting him. And then he told the Lord he thought the man deserved all that he got.

I kept glancing at the food, wishing he would come to a close. I nudged his leg with my knee, but he paid no attention, just kept on thanking the Lord. After about seven or eight more minutes of blessing the food, he said, "Amen."

When we had sat down all the food was good and hot, but he prayed so long it was now cold.

We were shown where to sleep. Then, after we each took a trip to the outhouse, we went to bed for a good night's sleep.

The wagon was unloaded during the night. The next morning, at the crack of dawn, I was at the barn, feeding and brushing the big mules. Soon I heard the clanging of the circular iron hanging near the kitchen. This was to let everyone know that the food was on the table.

I started towards the house and saw three big, black-bearded giants of men come carrying loaded sacks out of the hill behind the house. They passed me and continued on to my wagon.

I turned back a few steps so as to see what the men were doing. As I stood there, Mr. Anderson came to me and told me to be mighty careful going back to Harlan. He said, "Them men at your wagon are my brothers, and they are loading your wagon with moonshine to take back to Mr. Ford."

I went back to where the men were placing each jug throughout the wagon bed, cramming hay around each jug. After their sacks were emptied, we all went to eat breakfast.

Mr. Anderson said, "You have 400 gallons of liquor on your wagon, and I am going to arrange produce over it to conceal it." Some of the jugs contained molasses, for a fooler if I was searched going back. He placed sacks of shucky beans, dried apples, three or four bundles of furs, a few cowhides, and feed for my mules on the return trip.

We harnessed the mules and got ready to leave. Then Mrs. Anderson came from the house carrying a basket crammed full of food. Mr. Anderson came over to give me his instructions on the delivery of my load. I thanked them and told him I could handle it. This was not my first load of moonshine to take to Harlan.

As we were starting back across Kentucky Ridge, JoJo and I started ribbing Jesse about his religion. He said he "was trying to make a good impression on them folks," and that he intended to continue hauling over the mountain.

When we arrived at Mr. Lisenbee's, he and his family had the other wagons loaded with just about everything that could be raised and hunted. Several coops of nice fat hens, big lard cans filled with home-made lard, molasses, furs and hides. One wagon had 500 pounds of dried beef, big cases of honey, and lots more goods. Mr. Lisenbee said, "I will settle with Mr. Ford for hauling this stuff over the mountain." He was to travel with us on horseback.

The next evening late we made camp at the foot of Pine Mountain. As darkness was near, we heard wagons moving to camp. Dad, Jim, and Dave Good had arrived. We had a big fire going when they drove into camp. We helped them unhitch and care for their horses.

We gathered around the fire with our food baskets. We had plenty to eat without cooking, although we did make coffee. After a lot of tales were told, we got out our snoogins and crawled under the wagons to sleep.

Pretty soon, Dave came over to my wagon, knelt down, and asked me if I had a load of goods for Mr. Ford. I said I did, and then he told me he wanted me to take the last place going over the mountain. He had gotten word of revenuers planning to search our wagons. I was not loaded very heavy and I would have no trouble lagging way behind. We sat there and planned ourselves for any kind of an encounter with the revenuers.

The next morning as we all shuffled about hooking up for the

16

mountain crossing, I circled the camp a few times, limbering my big blacks up, planning on falling in last. JoJo was driving the big Percherons just ahead of me. We each had to do our own scotching. It was a lot steeper on this side of the mountain, but all the wagons were loaded light and we had no trouble making it to the top.

Dave told all the drivers to go ahead, that he would remain on top until I got there, but to make camp at the foot of the mountain. As I topped the mountain, about an hour behind the others, Dave was there waiting for me. We checked my load. It had shifted around a lot but none of the jugs had broken. The hides, beans, and furs had to be put into a better covering to hide the bottom of my load.

When all this was done we rough locked a rear wheel on each wagon and started down the mountain. We got to the big flat, and when we were about two-thirds through it, Dave held out his hand for me to stop. He came back to me and said, "The revenuers are just ahead, searching the wagons." We checked my load again and it was still in good shape. He said, "We just might as well move on down to them."

We came to a halt just behind Jesse's wagon. The officer in charge asked Dave if he was wagon master of this train. Dave answered, "Yes, I am. Why have you stopped the wagons?"

The officer said, "I have warrants to permit me to search each wagon that is under a Mr. David Good. He handed the warrant to Dave for him to read. After doing so, he asked the officer if anything was found in the wagons ahead. The officer said there wasn't.

Dave told the officer to feel free to continue his search. The officer raised the tail flap on Dave's wagon, looked in at all the furs and hides and saw nothing but them and a few country cured hams and middlins hanging throughout the wagon.

The officer looked at Dave and said, "Looks like the issuers of this warrant have been misinformed." He called ahead to pass the word to move on.

The officer asked Dave to sell him one of the big cured hams. Dave let him pick the one he wanted, for two dollars. It looked like it might weigh about forty-five or fifty pounds. He wrapped it for the officer in an old feed sack. The officer thanked him, then rode off after the rest of the revenuers.

I sure was proud of the way Dave handled this. He didn't appear to be excited or afraid of anything. He talked with the revenuer and just acted like he was happy to see him. He told him he had stayed behind to help me tack a couple of shoes on the mules. This being a rough and rocky road, he feared the mules would slip or crack a hoof. He didn't want any of the stock hurt that was under his command. This seemed to satisfy the officer. He looked back at me before he mounted, and called out for me to be careful coming on down the mountain.

It was right at dark when we arrived at the campsite. We all hustled about, ungearing our teams and making ready for camp. The first driver coming off the mountain had tied a good sized load of tree limbs behind his wagon and had dragged them to the center of our circle of wagons. When all the stock had been fed, watered, and brushed down good, we lit our fire and started making our supper. In just a few minutes everyone was drinking strong black coffee. Some of the men were eating from their possibles and others were toasting and browning sidemeat and roasting potatoes. It was a fairly good meal. We had just about used up all our grub.

The next morning, after a good night's sleep, we were eager to hitch up the teams and head for town. We gave the stock a little grain; they had about six or seven miles yet to go. The most of the way into town was in creek beds or creek banks rutted by wagon wheels.

As we came to the edge of town the wagons started turning off to stores and trading posts. I pulled my wagon up behind Mr. Ford's big house. JoJo pulled in behind me. Mr. Ford had seen us coming up the lane and was there to greet us. He helped ungear the teams, then we led them across the creek and turned them loose in the barn lot. I walked on over to the harness shed to see how the big Morgan was coming along. He was still hoisted, his front feet off the ground, just like he was when I left him. Mr. Ford had taken good care of Old Bob. His hoof had been bound tight and there was hardly any swelling at all. His body glistened from all the rubbing and brushing he had been given. After walking around him, patting and rubbing his nose, we went back to the wagons to unload them.

When Mrs. Ford asked if we were hungry, I told her, "We haven't eaten anything since the night before." She led us through the house to the kitchen. They had already had their dinner. Mrs. Ford started setting bowls of food and a big pitcher of cold sweet milk on the table. We didn't have to be told twice to go ahead and eat. Boy! JoJo could sure put away some food. He was about two years older than me, and close to thirty pounds heavier, and a lot meaner.

After we filled our bellies, Mr. Ford wanted a rundown of how the trip was. I explained to him about the driver abusing his team, and how we handled the problem of keeping the wagon rolling, and about Dave allowing JoJo to take over the driving.

Mr. Ford said, "You did an awful good job, and I am mighty thankful and pleased with the way you did your job." He started in telling about his driver coming back to town with his broken jaw, trying to get the sheriff to go after us. "The sheriff, after hearing him tell what it was all about, told him the best thing for him to do was to get whatever he owned and get the hell out of the county. There is a lot of mountain people around here that don't go in for beating work stock, and he personally didn't like the way he had flew into you."

Mr. Ford continued, "He told me he thought it would be best for him to go see Doc Cawood and have his jaw looked at. When he left the doctor's house, he came here to get what money he had coming to him. But he wouldn't tell me anything of what happened."

He got up and said, "We better unload the wagons." We had stopped the wagons near the cellar door. After removing all the furs, hides, and other stuff, we started carrying the jugs to a hidden side room in the cellar. We were very careful not to break any. Now, 400 one-gallon crock jugs to carry, two at a load down into the cellar and back up the steps, took us nearly three hours. JoJo and I were already tired.

We stopped to rest a spell and Mr. Ford asked me if I would like to own my own team and wagon. I said, "Sure would, but I would have to work and save until I got a lot of money." Mr. Ford said, "What about me letting you have that team of black mules and you working the price of them out with me? Say I hold a little money out of each job you do for me and then, on other jobs, you pay me a little of that. There is going to be a lot of hauling, all summer and fall. Some big street builders are moving into town to pave the streets. There's sand and gravel to haul from the river beds and shoals, and cement from railroad sidings."

I sat there, all eyes and ears, listening to him, with so much excitement growing in me I could hardly believe it was me he was talking to. He said, "You don't have to give me an answer until I talk to your dad, to see if it's all right for me to let you have them."

We got up to finish unloading the wagons. After we were finished, I asked Mr. Ford if me and JoJo could ride the mules home and let my younger brother and sister and Mom see them, and talk to Dad about it.

He said, "Sure, go ahead. But be back early in the morning."

19

THREE

JOJO AND I went to the barn, caught up the mules, and made a sack of hay to use as a saddle. We led them up to an old tree stump to climb on their backs.

Mr. Ford called for us to come by the house. He handed two sacks with the ends tied together up to JoJo and told him to drop them off at his home. Each sack was about half full of food—a big country ham in each sack, shucky beans, dried apples, and several jars— well wrapped—of huckleberries, jellies, and jams. He knew JoJo's family could use these things. Them living in town, they seldom got hold of good country food.

He then handed a loaded sack up to me. The bottom of the sack was filled part way with beans and potatoes just beginning to have sprouts on them. Snuggled between the potatoes, resting on top of the beans, he had placed a gallon jug of liquor. He told me to be careful and not let the mule trot, and to take the sack to his good friend, the sheriff. He gave me a second sack and said to tell the sheriff one of the sacks was for him and the other for his other good friend, the visiting revenuer.

The sheriff was out back of his house, raking and piling last year's weeds and leaves, getting his garden ready to be plowed. He saw me riding up and came over and asked me how the trip over the mountain was. I skipped around some parts that I didn't want to talk about and tried to tell him of things that he would not be interested in. I was just plain nervous, sitting there explaining to him.

I told him I had brought him a sack of stuff from Mr. Ford's. He reached up and helped me slide it from the mule's back. He thanked me and said maybe he could do something for me someday. He didn't know it right then, but it wasn't to be too long until he got the chance. I thanked him and said I'd better be heading for home.

We crossed the river going over to JoJo's home. His Mom and

all his younger brothers and sisters ran out to meet us. We rode our mules up to the house and he handed the sacks of food down, then he slid off the mule's back. His mother grabbed him up and hugged him and kissed his cheek, and the smaller children were clinging to him, asking a thousand questions at one time. JoJo handed me the bridle reins of the mule he had ridden, and I headed for home.

When I got within sight of home, I could see Mom and the girls coming from the milk gap. They saw me coming and set their milk pails down and came running down to meet me.

Artie wanted to lead the other mule. I gave her the bridle reins and we walked the mules up to the front yard. Dad and Jim were in the house eating supper. They heard all the kids jabbering and the big mules snorting and came out to see what was going on. I asked Jim to help me make room for the mules down at the cow barn and I would explain everything when we got through.

Mom told Artie to fix me a plate of food. As I sat there eating my supper, I started in telling the family about Mr. Ford's offer to let me buy the big blacks and a nearly new set of harness and how I was to pay him as I worked. Dad looked across the table at me and said, "You would have to go to school in the fall."

We were not going to do much planting, as there was plenty of work for him and his teams to do in town. He thought I might be able to do a lot of hauling and pay Mr. Ford a goodly part of the $300. We sat there and discussed it for a while and Dad said, "We'll go in the morning to talk with Mr. Ford."

The next morning Dad told Jim to go ahead with the planned work they were to do. Dad kept his teams at the big livery barn in the edge of town and used riding horses to go and come from home. We rigged sacks of hay to use as saddles and Dad and I took off on the big mules. We arrived at Mr. Ford's about the time that his drivers were hitching their teams. We turned the mules into the barn lot and went with Mr. Ford to the house.

When we were seated, Mrs. Ford brought me a glass of milk. She brought a brown jug and empty glasses for Dad and Mr. Ford. Mr. Ford told her to take the milk away and give me an empty glass. He said that he thought I'd become man enough to drink like one. This sure made me feel proud, to have a man like him to speak of me like that. He told Dad he should thank his Lord for giving him sons like Jim and me.

Jim, being a little older than me, was always the apple of Dad's eye. It seemed like when discussing things around home that I was never included in anything. Listening to Dad, Mom, and Jim making plans for the future, I made up my mind that if I ever was to have anything, it would be of my own planning.

I sat there, listening to them discuss ways for me to work the team and try to go to school in the fall. They got me to agree to keep the mules at the livery stable, and Mr. Ford assured me that I would get all the hauling I could do until school started. I could hire Jesse to drive for me during the winter months. With a few trips over the mountains for him, everybody would be happy and my big blacks would be getting good care.

Dad agreed for me to make the deal with Mr. Ford, we all shook hands, and that was all the contract there was. When you shook hands with a mountain man, it meant that his honor was bound with that handshake. We got up from the table and started to the door. I turned to Dad and asked if I could have the other drink that Mr. Ford had poured for me earlier.

I would not be thirteen years old until July, but I was being talked to and treated like a man. I thought a little drink of whiskey would bolster some of the shock out of me. I'd sipped from a lot of jugs, but this was the largest drink of liquor I had ever drunk. I got sick before we got to the livery stable, but I didn't tell anyone.

It was all decided that the deal was made and I was to take charge of the big blacks as of now. We shook hands again and me and Dad harnessed them to the big wagon and drove into town.

We stopped at the livery stable and I paid the hostler for one month's feed and stall space, which cost me nearly all the money I had. Mr. Ford had paid me good for making the trips across the mountain and for getting his moonshine to him. He also gave me $10.00 to give to JoJo.

I left Dad at the livery stable and drove my team on up to town. I pulled up to the sheriff's house and tied the big blacks down, then looked around the house for the sheriff. He was finishing cleaning his garden off.

I asked him to come and look at my own team. Now, the sheriff was a man of no fooling around with. He knew me and all the rest of my family by our first names. Every fall he would find out when we were butchering hogs and would come and help. He always wanted a hog's head, liver, lungs, and feet. His wife would make loaf from these and call it head cheese.

After looking the team and wagon over, I told him Mr. Ford had agreed to let me buy them on credit and I had come to him to find out if he could help me sign on to haul sand and gravel for the street builders. He said, "I sure would." He climbed up in the wagon and we drove to the railroad depot.

The foreman was there, unloading road-building machinery. The sheriff called him over to us and explained what we were doing there. The foreman kept walking around my big mules and admiring the big heavy wagon.

The foreman said he believed that was the finest looking outfit he ever saw. He asked me if I could start work today. I said I could. He then directed me to the railroad flatcars loaded with heavy pieces of machinery. He wanted them moved to where he had started building streets.

I drove and backed the wagon to the side of the car. He sent three big strong men to work with me. It took four trips to haul the machinery to where he wanted it. On the last trip I called to the foreman and told him that this load emptied the car. He then told me to come prepared for a ten-hour work day every day and told me how much money the company paid a day. I was allowed $3.00 a day for each mule and $2.00 a day for my wagon when I used it, and $2.50 a day for myself. The foreman warned me that it would be hard work for me and the mules. Some days the mules would be worked single, but he would pay for the extra driver.

I could just see the money rolling in. I asked him if I could get the extra driver for him to hire. He said, "That would be just fine." We unloaded this last load for the day.

I left my wagon where we unloaded it and walked my team over to the livery stable. The hostler said he would feed, water, groom, and have my mules harnessed for me every morning by the time I got there. The extra charge for this was $3.00 a week. I told him that if he would keep my harness repaired, it would be a deal. That suited him fine.

It was yet early, about four o'clock. I thought I should go around by JoJo's home and ask him if he would like to work on the street job. He said, "You're joking me. They are not hiring but big grown men!"

I told them they had hired my team and myself and I had spoken to the foreman about him to drive one of my mules. JoJo's face lit up with a big smile. He pulled me into the house, skipped over and hugged his mother and told her what I had said. Mrs. Walters came over and gave me a big hug and kissed me on the cheek.

I got home about dark. Dad and Jim were just setting down to their supper. Mom had put the smaller children to bed. She told Artie to set me a plate.

Not much talk went on while we were eating. Artie had cooked a good supper. We had a good size helping of pickled beans and corn and a big platter of golden brown fried chicken, hot biscuits, and a steaming pan of huckleberry cobbler with a pitcher of sweet dip to pour over it.

I thought it strange to have such a big meal like this in the middle of the week. As we sat there, finishing the last of the cobbler, I glanced past Dad's shoulder and there stood Artie with her boyfriend Amos, with a big smile on her face. Artie came around to where she looked at Dad's face. Standing there, holding hands with Amos, she told Dad that she and Amos had gotten married this morning.

Dad pushed back from the table and got up to shake hands with Amos. Amos, thinking Dad was reaching to grab him, broke loose from Artie's hand and ran through the door to the back porch. Artie was screaming for Dad not to hurt him. Amos could not stop at the edge of the porch, he cleared the porch railing and hit the ground running.

Artie called after Amos to stop and come back, but there was no stopping him. He was one scared boy. Artie came back in with tears running down her face. Dad told her that all he meant to do was to shake hands with Amos and welcome him to the family.

After Artie had composed herself, Dad told her that he would go bring Amos back. She asked if she could go with him. Jim went to saddle the two horses and led them up to the yard. Dad helped Artie to mount, then stepped into his saddle. Mom handed him a lantern and they took off down the mountain.

Mom gave me and Jim a rundown of what had happened earlier in the day. I sat there with a thousand things running through my head. Artie was the only one in my family that would listen to my likes and dislikes. Sometimes she would sit and talk with me for hours about how she thought we two were different from the other children.

As Mom was clearing the table, I just sat there like I was in a daze, but my mind was trying to work out what Artie had always talked to me about. Mom never seemed to care if I was warm or if I felt sick. She paid it no mind. It was always Artie who would mix up medicine and herbs to check a cold or cough. It was Artie that would bandage and bathe an injure that I would get from time to time. All this was running through my head, not knowing what I would do when she left us to make a home for herself.

My brother Jim had gone on to bed and Mom was still working around in the kitchen. Finally she got through and came over to sit down in front of me. We just sat there staring at each other. I was tall, well boned, and strong as an ox. Mom started talking to me and I could hardly believe it was me she was talking to.

I came out of my daze as she was telling me she thought I was big enough and old enough to be told a lot of things I should know. She started off by telling me why Artie was always closer to me and loved me more than she did any of the others. I was wise enough about the facts of life to know what she was about to tell me. I asked her to not talk about it any more, that I thought I knew what she was going to tell me.

About that time I heard Dad and Artie's horses coming up the hill, their iron shoes sounding against the rocks. Then I could hear Amos telling Dad how scared he was when Dad rose from the table to shake hands. They both laughed about it.

Amos was riding in the saddle and Artie was riding behind him. Me and Mom were standing on the porch as they rode up in the yard. After dismounting, Dad told me to tend to the horses. When I got back to the house they were sitting at the table, having a glass of milk and a piece of a molasses cake Artie had baked.

I drug me out a chair and sat away from the table, listening to them talk. When they had quieted down, I said, "I would like to tell you about me hiring on with the street builders."

Dad didn't have much to say about it, but he told me I would have to be on my own. He had all he could handle. He said if it wasn't for the help Jim gave him he couldn't keep his own teams going.

I never could understand why he would never tell me to handle a team. It was always him and Jim to make the main decisions on everything. As I sat there, I could feel every pulse in my body go tense. Artie had got married, Mom had started to tell me things I wished she hadn't started, and now Dad was telling me that I was more useless around him than a stranger.

Artie and Amos stood there. Tears started to swell in Artie's eyes. She looked first to Mom, then to Dad, with an expression on her face that I'll remember till my dying day. Amos was getting to see the dark side of his new family.

After Dad got through talking I just sat there, trying to believe what I had just heard. I could not bring myself to be humble to him or Mom. But I wanted to say something to Artie or do something to let her know that I was in a position to care for myself. And I could leave the mountain this night and never feel regret for doing so.

I thought of all this so strong that I all at once realized I was standing in front of Dad, telling him all I had been thinking. When I was through, I just stood there, expecting to be slapped or cuffed about. But Dad, with a cool, smooth voice, told Mom to see to it that I would not be there in the morning. Then he turned to go to his bedroom.

Artie and Amos came over to me and said they would go with me. I told them no, for them to stay until tomorrow, then come to JoJo's home. I thought that's where I might be.

Mom came down from the attic with a big paper sack and laid it at my feet. She said she thought that was all the clothes I had.

It was close to ten o'clock when I left, and it was one of the darkest nights I can ever remember. I stumbled several times over big rocks and washed-out places, hardly noticing it when I fell.

I hit the ground, reaching out to grasp something. My hand caught hold of an old piece of barb wire. The barb dug into the palm of my hand, causing a deep gash about two inches long. I just sat there for a while, then I burst loose and let the tears come. I had kept them back until now.

I don't recall how long I sat there, wiping my eyes and trying to stop my hand from bleeding. Finally, after my eyes seemed to clear up and my hand felt like it had stopped bleeding, I got up and continued to feel my way off the mountain.

FOUR

IT WAS ABOUT three o'clock when I knocked on Mrs. Walters' door. She woke JoJo to answer the door. He lit an oil lamp, then called out to ask who was there. I told him. He swung the door open and saw me standing there with blood over the most of my clothes. And my eyes, I knew he could tell they had been flooded.

JoJo pulled me into the house and called his mother to come quick and told her, "Somebody has tried to kill Red." She came rushing in and nearly fainted when she saw all the blood on me. All the time I was trying to tell what had happened, but with both of them jabbering at the same time, it took several minutes to explain to them.

Mrs. Walters bathed and bound my hand and got the bloody clothes taken off. JoJo, wide awake, kept wanting to know why I was there at this time of night. I told him to go back to bed and I would tell him all about it in the morning.

Mrs. Walters put some old quilts on an old folding army cot and told me to lay down and try to get to sleep. She then blew out the light, and I slept good.

They let me sleep until six o'clock. I got up, put on some clean overalls and a new shirt she had made for another one of her sons. I washed my face in cold water and held a handful of it to my eyes to help kill the stinging and redness I knew were in them.

Breakfast was on the table and the aroma from a big plate of country ham was sure getting to me. Mrs. Walters had made a big mound of steaming hot biscuits, a bowl of gravy, eggs, butter, and country wild honey.

I had to eat in a hurry. I didn't want to be late on my first day on my new job. I asked if JoJo could go with me. Mrs. Walters tried to get me to let JoJo go tell the foreman I had an accident, but she did let him go with me. She wrapped up some ham, biscuits, eggs, and a little honey in a cloth and told us to eat it for lunch.

When we got to the livery stable, Uncle John, the hostler (no kin to me, everybody called him Uncle) had the big blacks harnessed. They had been brushed till they shined like they had been polished. Uncle John sure loved to care for good animals. We were the first to leave the stable. Other drivers were brushing and harnessing their stock.

Dad and Jim came riding up. Jim came to a stop and asked what happened to my hand. Dad rode on into the stable, paying me no mind. I told Jim how I hurt it. He cursed Dad and Mom and all he thought had anything to do with it.

Me and JoJo led the mules to where I had left my wagon. I was still a little groggy and red eyed from last night and my hand wasn't letting up. It ached and pained like a toothache. The boss, Ben Howard, came up to give out orders for the day's work and saw me holding my bandaged hand up on the other shoulder. He asked me what was wrong. I told him I had snagged it on a wire. I asked him if JoJo could drive instead of me and told him that JoJo was the one I was to bring for him to meet. The boss walked over to JoJo and shook hands and said he would be pleased to hire him. JoJo's eyes gleamed with pride as he came over to where I stood. Mr. Howard said JoJo would be working as a company hired man and the company would pay his wages. I would be paid my rate just to stay on the job.

JoJo hitched the big mules to the wagon and I climbed up to sit beside him. Three other workers got in the wagon to ride to the railroad siding. The foreman was there waiting. There were three huge pieces of machinery on a flatcar he wanted to be placed at different spots throughout the town. They were too large to put in the wagon. After measuring a dozen times or more the foreman gave up and said he would have to dismantle them to move them. I looked at my big blacks and then at the machinery. I asked the foreman if I could make a suggestion. He said, "Go ahead."

There were some big stacks of heavy sawed timber where I had left my wagon last night and I wanted to get about six or seven pieces of it to make a skid, then work the machinery off onto it and hitch my team to the skid and drag the load anywhere he wanted it.

The foreman wanted to know how in the hell why he hadn't thought of doing that. I said, "I guess it's because you're not a mountain man. We up in these hills try to make do with what we have."

He laughed at that and said he had some other things to do and for me to go ahead and get it done. He also told the work crew with me that I would be in charge and to do everything I asked them to do. We had no trouble at all moving the pieces to where they were to be used.

My hand hardly hurt at all since the foreman put me in charge of the job. I guess a lot of the remedy came from walking through town behind two of the finest big black mules that ever walked them streets. They sure made me feel proud.

When we got back to the wagon it was lunch time. JoJo watered the blacks and gave them some feed in a nose bag. Then we spread our lunch out on the tailgate of the wagon and started in on that ham and biscuits. JoJo's mom sure knew how to feed a working man. I'd already agreed with myself that I was no longer a kid. I was tall as some of the men working with me, and about as strong.

JoJo was doing a good job handling the big blacks, and I told him so. The foreman came up as we finished eating and fingered into our lunch cloth and got a thick slice of ham, placed a fried egg on it, opened one of Mrs. Walters's big biscuits up, and made him a sandwich. He sure enjoyed it.

The foreman was pleased with the way I had moved the machinery. He started telling me what he wanted the team to do. The rest of the day I was to drive to the hardware and pick up two slip scrapers and start grading ditch lines. He had a large black man to handle the loading of the scrapers and another colored man to drive one of the mules.

I wanted to hold this job, but I didn't intend for him to kill my mules, working them single to a half-yard scraper. I told him my mules worked as a team, not single. He tried to haggle me into letting him try it for the rest of the day. I said, "No," and told JoJo to hitch the team to the wagon.

Then the foreman held up his hand and said, "Wait a minute there!" He explained he worked for a hard company and it wanted all the work he could get from man or beast. But he sure as hell didn't want me to quit. He said, "You work them mules just the way you want to, for I know you'll do a good day's work." That settled that dispute.

I worked my mules like that until my hand healed, about three weeks. JoJo was making a top-notch mule skinner. He had them mules minding every command he called. The foreman managed to be around when lunch time came. He would talk with the men and sorta sidle over to where me and JoJo were eating and say something about how bad the food was at the boarding house. This always got him a big juicy sandwich and a cup of cold buttermilk.

My sister Artie and my new brother-in-law came to see about me the next day after Mom packed my clothes. Artie told Mrs. Walters what had happened that night and said that just as soon as she could get settled in the little house they were furnishing that day, she wanted me to stay with her. I hadn't moved in with her yet, and that had been a little over three weeks.

This being Sunday morning, me and JoJo were at the stable fooling around, grooming the big blacks. We got paid the day before and we were strutting around in brand-new overalls and store-bought shirts and new work shoes. I had enough money to pay for another month's stable rent and I paid Uncle John what I owed already. He was taking care of my mules like they were his.

Out of my three weeks' pay Mrs. Walters had helped me save $85 to pay Mr. Ford. After JoJo and I groomed the mules until they shined like black glass, we rode them out to Mr. Ford's. He was tending the big Morgan. Big Bob was still in the sling, his front feet off the ground. The bone had healed good. The hoof was not well but it was doing fairly good.

Mr. Ford finished dressing the hoof, then asked us over to the house. It being nearly dinner time I was hoping we could talk around about something until Mrs. Ford would invite us to have dinner with them. We sat on the porch and I counted out the $85 to him. He asked if I wanted a written receipt. I said, "No, just a handshake will do fine."

He said he had heard of what happened, about me being thrown from home. "I can't understand it."

I said, "You could, if you knew my people like I know them."

We heard Mrs. Ford call from the kitchen that dinner was on the table and for him to bring JoJo and me along. That suited me fine. Now, Mrs. Ford set a mighty fine table. There were at least twenty different things to eat on that table. As I've told you before, that boy JoJo could sure put away some food.

When we started to leave, Mr. Ford asked if I would take a couple of bags of home-ground meal to the sheriff. I said, "I sure would."

We went down into the cellar and he got out two long meal sacks and put about a peck of cornmeal in each sack, then placed two one-gallon jugs of liquor in each sack. Then, tying the ends of the sack, he shook about half the meal to the tied end of the sack and snugly eased a jug to each end, with the meal fitting around the jug. It appeared like we were carrying nothing but cornmeal. We mounted our mules and Mr. Ford eased our sacks of cornmeal up to us. We walked the mules slowly back to town, skirting the main parts where people would be gathered to do their Sunday horse trading and swapping.

Talk of how fast the surrounding county was growing! New coal mining companies were coming into our county. It seemed like a mine would open up and be producing coal overnight, and all the workers were strangers to these hills. A lot of them came from as far away as Italy, and I met a few who said they were from Scotland, Ireland, and England. I tell you, these big thick seams of coal discovered here were being talked about all over the world. It was hard for our small town to meet all the demands the new people were making.

As we moved along the back streets, making our way to the sheriff's house, we met Dad and Jim riding their slick, shiny saddles. As we came to a stop Jim asked me how my hand was. I pulled my arm outside my overall bibb and showed him. It had scabbed over good and hadn't left any scar hardly at all. Dad sat there on his horse, glancing our way, not saying anything.

Jim said, "We are going to look at a logging job. A big sawmill has set up at a little village called Baxter and they want Dad to contract the logging."

Dad asked me if I wanted to come along. I shook my head that I didn't, remembering what he had told Mom the night I left the mountain.

He said to Jim, "We had better be moving on, if we want to get back home before dark."

They took off at a fast pace and JoJo and I continued on to the sheriff's home. He was out puttering around in his garden. He sure did raise himself a fine lot of vegetables. We rode up to his fence and I told him Mr. Ford had sent him some cornmeal. We eased the sacks off the mules and the sheriff reached across the fence. He handled them carefully to lay by a fencepost. He then asked me how I was coming along on my job. He said he had been hearing a lot of the town people tell about how JoJo and me were doing such a fine job for the street building company. He said, "I'm very proud to have helped you hire on to the contractors." I thanked him for what he had done. The sheriff looked up to JoJo and said, "I've been hearing a lot of good talk about you." It always brought a big, toothy grin from JoJo to have someone to speak kindly of him. We told the sheriff good-bye and rode the big black mules through the main part of town, heading back to the livery stable.

A lot of the new people were gathered around the store fronts, making new friends and introducing their pretty wives and their babies to the town people and shop owners. As we rode through, a lot would say admiring remarks about what beautiful mules we were riding.

After stabling the mules, we paused awhile with Uncle John. He wanted us to have a bottle of pop and a big chocolate bar of candy. I'll never forget the name of that candy bar. It had nuts all through it, the center was caramel, and the outside seemed like it had a half inch of the sweetest dark, nearly black chocolate all around it. The bar was called "O. Henry."

Uncle John told me to go on home and leave the feeding and brushing of the blacks to him. He said, "I am beginning to love to care for them." That sure made me feel good and thankful to him, knowing they were getting the care of such a fine person.

When we got to Mrs. Walters', they were having supper. She hustled around to set JoJo and me plates. We had a good helping of chicken and dumplings, left over from dinner. We sat there and nearly busted a gut. It seemed like eating was all we did on Sundays.

The next day, about ten o'clock, the foreman came around where we were ditching. I had decided the mules would not be too overworked pulling a scraper single. JoJo was driving one, me the other one. After all, Ben Howard was such a good man to work for. I had been given over three weeks' pay for doing nothing but hanging around the job, and him letting me allow JoJo to drive.

We were circling them mules, just like clockwork. Round and round we went. Mr. Howard pulled over to the side and said, "What in the hell do you mean working with your hand still sore?" I showed him how it had healed up but was yet still sore and tender. He said for me to put another man driving and get my ass up on the bank and stay there.

The boss liked the way we had the ditching going and working the mules single. He said, "I'll let you know when I want you to do anything other than see to the work going on with your mules."

We worked like this on through June. The big blacks were doing fine, working single.

While eating lunch this Saturday on the last week of June, JoJo said to Mr. Howard that I had a birthday coming the tenth of July and I would be thirteen years old. Mr. Howard said, "I thought he was closer to thirty-one instead of thirteen, the way he is handling his job. I have never seen a job run any smoother than the way he is handling this one."

The work continued on until July the ninth. Mr. Howard told me to knock off at noon and be at his office by six o'clock. JoJo took the team to the livery and I went to Mrs. Walters'. I took a bath, although it wasn't Saturday, the usual night for bathing. Mrs. Walters kept all my clothes clean and ironed. By now I had several changes of clothes. I picked me out a nice pair of overalls and a blue checkered shirt I had bought me and a nice pair of shiny black boots.

I did all this and headed for the office. There were about a dozen horses standing tied to the fencepost at the rear of the office. I knocked on the door. Someone said, "Come in," and I entered. Seated all around in the room were men I had never seen. I stood there for a moment and Mr. Howard got up from his desk, came over, and stood beside me. Me dressed in my clean clothes and my red hair laying anyway but the right way. And he said, "Gentlemen, I'd like you to meet my very good friend and one of your employees."

All the men but one, an elderly gentleman, stood up and one of them asked if I was the man Ben and the sheriff had been telling them about. He said, "He's nothing but a kid."

Ben said, "Hold on, this kid is more of a man than I or you will ever be. I've asked you here to check my progress on this job. Tomorrow he'll be thirteen years old and he has been my assistant on all the ditching and draining, and moving the larger pieces of machinery. He also owns the finest team of big black mules you ever saw."

They just stood there, looking at me. Mr. Howard, Ben's dad, the elderly gentleman and the president of the company, stood up and said, "I am very proud of the work Ben has got done in such a short time, and the low cost it is amounting to." On the evening before, the good sheriff, with Ben and himself, had ridden over the entire area we had worked on and found what was done was very commendable on my part.

The other men standing there stared at me like I was some kind of a freak, and to tell you the truth I felt like one. I hadn't spoken one word. I guess I was what you might call in a state of shock. When I came out of it, some of the men were swarming all around me, shaking my hand and slapping me on the back. Jonathan Evers, the one who had jumped up and called me just a kid said, "Someday I'll learn to keep my damn mouth shut."

We were all introduced to each other by full name and each man explained his position and power in the company. After all the extra handshaking and introductions, Mr. Howard, Ben's father, suggested they proceed with the evening's plans.

I got up from my seat that was given to me by Jonathan Evers. I started towards the door and said, "I had better be getting on."

Ben said, "No, you're still my employee and you're having your supper with us over at the boarding house."

The boarding house was a huge building. There must have been thirty-five or forty rooms in it. We entered a long, wide sitting room. A lot of the people I had seen around town were lolling around in big cushioned chairs and feeling completely at ease. Just then a bell rang and all the people got up and went to the dining room. Ben took hold of my arm and whispered to me to stop shaking, as he led me to the dining room.

One big long table in the back is where he led me. We were all standing at the table when Mr. Howard asked us to be seated. We sat down to the most beautiful table I had ever seen. It was completely covered with food, silverware, and pretty snow-white cloths. I sure wished Artie or any of my family could be there and see it.

Now, the only places I had ever eaten at were out in the country or a little two-by-four restaurant where you could buy hamburgers or hotdogs for a nickel. I didn't know any manners, so I had to watch Ben's movements and try to follow his way of eating.

First I dropped my white cloth, trying to place it under my chin. Then I spilled a big glass of milk. Next, my knife slid off my steak and upset my plate, turning it upside down in my lap. Everybody was staring at me.

I felt so bad about my actions I got up to leave. My foot slipped in the gravy that had been in my plate and I fell, turning my chair over. It hit Ben's shin. He jumped up, grabbing at his leg, and fell backwards into the lady that was carrying a large bowl of potatoes. She was shocked. She ran back to the kitchen. I ran out of there!

The next Monday morning we started working, everything going along smooth as ever. When Mr. Howard and Ben came by, Ben motioned for me to come to where he and his father were standing. Ben said, "They are stopping the job. No more money was appointed for the rest of the year. I have just been told this by the town clerk."

He wanted me to move all his machinery to a big lumber shed for storage, and when I got through, to come to the office and the bookkeeper would pay me up to date.

I got my check, looked at the figures, and told the lady there must have been a mistake made. She assured me that she was an experienced bookkeeper and very capable of keeping her office work straight. I thanked her and rushed to the bank to cash the check before it could be stopped. The check was made out for $100 more than was due me. After cashing the check, my conscience got to bothering me. I hunted Ben up and told him that I had tried to tell the bookkeeper of the mistake.

Ben said, "There wasn't any mistake. The extra money is yours as a bonus for the work you have done and for the repair you might need to do on your wagon and harness."

Man, I sure hadn't looked forward to anything like this. I owed Mr. Ford $65.00 and had seven weeks paid in advance at the livery stable and I had over $200.00 saved at Mrs. Walters'. I thought she was safer than a bank.

All the workers got their checks and started planning on going to Lexington, Kentucky. There was a lot of work going on down there.

The next morning, JoJo helped me hook the big blacks to the wagon and we drove to the wholesale to see about some hauling. They were planning on a small train of wagons to leave Thursday morning. The trip would pay me $90 going over and I could make a little extra coming back. I signed up for the trip.

Heavy wagons were getting scarce. The coal mines were opening up all over the county. The mine owners were hiring the wagons and promising to pay more than their present jobs would pay. For the rest of the summer and nearly all the fall I had more trips over the mountain than I wanted to make my mules pull.

FIVE

THE MULES were mine now. I had paid Mr. Ford all I owed him. They were beginning to slow up, not prancing as much. The hard work of pulling the scrapers was showing on them. I had the hostler to add more grain to their feeding and be sure they got their regular dosage of Dr. Legear's worm and kidney powder. Work stock have to be kept wormed. If their urine begins to look real golden, their kidneys are not right. They need to pass clear urine.

It was beginning to turn cool now. It was about the middle of October. The coal mines were idle, all the northern factories were closing. Nearly all the teamsters had left the coal mines and were taking any kind of hauling they could get.

I wanted to go to school this winter, but owning my team of mules and trying to keep JoJo with me, I couldn't see how I could manage to go to school and keep jobs lined up.

I was paying Mrs. Walters $9 a week for my keep, and $55 to the livery stable. The blacksmithing sometimes ran as high as $75 a month. Uncle John had stopped charging me for harnessing my mules. I had wasted over a hundred dollars buying two big western saddles from Uncle Hamp Huff, but JoJo and I got a lot of pleasure out of them. We would take a ride somewhere nearly every Sunday.

On November 15 we drove out to Mr. Ford's. It was butchering day. Let it come rain or shine, he would not fail to butcher on this day. He would hire four good strong men to help him. He would slaughter twenty to thirty big fat hogs and from six to eight beef cattle. The people in town depended on him for a lot of meat.

I drove into the wagon yard, tied my team down good, and thought I should look in on the lame Morgan. Nearly all the horses were in the barn or running in the lot, but I could not find Old Bob. I heard someone call from up on the hill above the barn. I looked up. There was Old Bob coming down the hill dragging a large bunched-up pile of poles behind him. He looked completely healed. The man behind him was calling out commands to him to go gee or haw, directing him to drag the load to where a big fire was blazing.

Mr. Ford and the other men had four big hogs dressed and hanging upside down from a big rafter log at the harness shed. They had three huge vats of water boiling. As they killed each hog, they would lower it into the boiling water, then raise it out and lay it on some large, wide boards, and Mr. Ford would start scraping and pulling the hair from the head. The other men, with long sharp knives, would begin scraping the feet. After the feet and head were cleaned, the hair on the hams, shoulders, and side would just about fall off. They kept thick feed sacks laying on these parts while they were cleaning the head and feet. Mr. Ford would be pouring scalding water over the sacks. It was something to watch, how smooth and skilled these people were, going about their work.

I had brought my wagon to haul the dressed beef back to town, to the town's only meat store. The five beefs I loaded were just about all my team could handle. I had some steep hills to go over.

The old man who owned the meat store was some kind of a foreigner. I think he might have been Hungarian or Greek. After we hung all the meat, the old butcher paid me for hauling it. He said, "I guess this will put me out of business. I've got all my money tied up in this meat and the United Mine Workers' Union have come out on strike. I just don't know what I'll do. I wish I hadn't left my country, but all I canna hear, 'go to America, go to America,' thisa all I canna hear. You wanna buya my shop?"

I sure felt sorry for that old man. He would let anybody buy all the meat they wanted, no matter if they had the money or not. He trusted them to pay when they got a job. Some of the men are living yet that owe that old man money for meat and other foodstuff that kept their families from starving. Some of these men are the wealthiest men there are in Harlan today.

The L. & N. Railroad serviced Harlan. They had put in miles and miles of sidetracks. Every one of them was filled with loaded coal cars. Nothing was being shipped out of Harlan.

For a while I thought logs—oak, walnut, poplar, pine, or just about any kind of hardwood logs—were in demand in Lexington, but now all the logging men just loafed around town. There was no work going on anywhere in the whole country. The big depression was near. The big businessmen in northern states were committing suicide over the sudden collapse of the stocks or the failure of their business.

Now, don't think I was living in a bed of roses myself. I had made real good pay hauling a few loads of staple goods over Pine Mountain and doing a little hauling around town. I kept the livery stable paid in advance. All other expenses I paid as I purchased them. Mrs. Walters had dropped from $9 a week to $5 a week. I wasn't using JoJo anymore, although he would go with me and work just like he was being paid for it. I'd slip him a dollar or two every now and then.

The weather was getting real cold. It lacked ten days till Christmas. Dad had sold all his stock to the sawmill company and he had not raised a crop the past summer. I knew that he had paid all his debts with the money he received from selling his stock. He still had two riding horses and two good milk cows, and chickens were plentiful—they were just about wild. The chickens would scrodge for all kinds of mast, like fallen nuts, berryseed, tender roots from weeds and underbrush that grew in back of the barn. They would roost in and around the barn. When Mom wanted a chicken for the next day's meal it was no trouble to take her pick from hundreds roosting in the barn.

I knew none of them would go hungry, but they had no money or anything to bring to town to sell. With Christmas near I got to thinking about the other children. Here I was, on my own, with nearly three hundred dollars that Mrs. Walters was keeping for me, and I didn't owe a cent to anyone. I asked Mrs. Walters if I should try to manage for Artie and Amos to take some of my money and buy my family some things for Christmas. Mrs. Walters said, "That would be the greatest Christmas you would ever have, if your Dad and Mom would allow it."

I walked across town to where Artie and Amos lived. They were getting their evening chores done, carrying water from a big spring that kept seeping under a large white oak tree. No family would go to bed until there were several pails of water in the house. They saw me and waved for me to come on up. They were pleased to have me visit them. Their house was small, three rooms with a large front porch and a small porch at the kitchen. Amos, being raised in the mountains, knew how to make do with what he had. When the work stopped at the coal mines he started laying up foodstuff for the hard days ahead.

Artie had her house filled with beautiful furniture. The walls were papered with real store-bought wallpaper. This room where we were sitting was the kitchen. Amos had built pretty cupboards with glass doors, and put shelves all along the walls. Artie had made pretty curtains and put around the shelves. The walls were papered with a design I had never seen. It showed all kinds of dishes of food, some with little streamers of steam coming from them. About every kind of vegetable you could think of was scattered throughout the whole design. It had designs of fruit too, with bunches of grapes hanging over the edges of big wooden bowls, and nuts of every kind in the world heaped in the center of them. Artie was sitting there, just beaming with pride, as I went all around the kitchen, asking her what the names of a lot of the fruits and vegetables were. Some of them were as foreign to me as daylight is to dark.

When I sat down Artie brought out a big pineapple upside-down cake and a pitcher of cold sweet milk. We sat there enjoying it to the last crumb. It was my favorite cake, and still is.

Artie and Amos, sitting there with pleased and happy looks on their faces, asked if I would come and stay Christmas night with them. I told them my visit was to find out if Artie thought I should get the family something for Christmas. Although I had been disowned by them, I couldn't help but have an inside love for all of them.

As I was talking, my mind was drifting back to the time Dad had knelt down beside the man with the broken jaw and had told him if he ever laid a hand on one of his kids he would kill him. The more I thought about it, the more I thought that he might have a little love for me. I had always obeyed everything he told me, but sometimes I would think that he wanted me to not be near him, or maybe that he and Jim or Mom wanted to discuss something.

All of this was flashing through my mind as we sat there and Artie was writing down what she would get for each one. Dad was to have a pair of high-cut, laced dress boots, with a pair of tan riding pants and a pair of soft leather gloves. Jim was to have the same, and both the same color.

For my two younger brothers, William and Dave, she was to get some good warm underwear, overalls, and each one a pair of boots with a jack knife in a little pocket sewed on the side of one of them.

Narciss and Sophia were to get warm coats. They called these coats "chinchillas." They had a pretty little piece of fur around the collar and a small ring of fur at the end of each sleeve. The coats were to be different colors. They had never worn town shoes, so Artie said, "I will try to find each one a pretty pair."

Artie wanted to get for Mom a nice set of dishes and two store-bought dresses. She would get bags of fruit and a few pounds of foreign-grown nuts and a lot of Christmas colored candy for her to put in the children's Christmas socks.

Artie's eyes started watering. She came over and hugged me and said, "I thought I had loved you before, but that was no love at all compared to the way I love you now." I started welling up a little myself, looking at her, and rubbed my eyes a few times to clear them up.

I had brought $200 for her to spend. She thought that was far too much, that $125 would be plenty. I told her to take it all, that I had a lot more and didn't owe anything and for her to keep what she didn't spend, for her and Amos.

If her eyes were watering before, they were flowing like streams now. I told her to keep it in return for all the kind things she had done for me back home. She agreed to do as I asked her. I got up to leave. They followed me to the door, wanting me to stay the night with them. I said, "I have to get an early start in the morning," and then I left.

It was now dark. I trudged across town to Mrs. Walters'. I got to thinking of all the times I had been shoved aside, sent out of the house to do things that I knew were of no use at all. They just didn't want me near them. The more I thought of this, the more I thought I was just trying to buy my way back home. But that was not it. I still loved them all and missed being around them.

The next morning the H.T. Hackney Wholesale wanted me to put the cover on my wagon and load up that afternoon for a trip to the Pine Mountain School. I was to park my loaded wagon in the hallway of the livery stable overnight. They wanted me to get an early start in the morning so I could arrive a day before Christmas. I got JoJo to make the trip with me.

The mountains were rough, with a lot of washed-out places all along the way. My big blacks were in fine shape, getting prettier and shinier every day. I kept my wagon painted, greased, and all the bolts tightened, for I never knew when I would be called on to make a haul over the mountain.

We made it to the school as scheduled, without too much trouble. After spending the night in one of the student cabins, we slipped out, geared the blacks, and took off for Harlan. We went back empty and made good time over the mountain.

Artie had done a good job getting the Christmas things on the mountain. Dad and Jim were away, so Artie and Amos hid all the Christmas gifts in the cellar. The next morning they all got up to the greatest Christmas they had ever had. Their socks were filled with all kinds of goodies and they put their new clothes on. Then Mom and Dad asked Artie where it all came from. I had told her to not tell them it was from me until they had accepted everything. Dad had been brooding over not being able to buy things for Christmas. Artie said all my brothers and sisters were excited and thrilled over getting so many gifts, and they all were asking about me.

Mom opened her new dishes and they ate breakfast on them. Dad sat over near the big kitchen window, looking off down the hill. Then turning to Amos he said, "I wished my son was here." Artie said he had a sad look on his face, and when Mom told him to come to breakfast, he just sat there, looking off down the mountain.

While Artie was telling me all this, my brain was traveling a thousand miles a minute. Artie said, "You should go and see them." She thought they were sorry about the way they had made me leave the mountain.

My Christmas was spent coming back across Pine Mountain. I got so cold when we started down that I thought I was going to freeze. I had to sit up in the seat and control the brake and hold the checkreins, not being able to move around much. My long-johns were wet from sweating while coming up the other side. I thought I was wearing a sheet of ice wrapped around me.

JoJo was walking behind the wagon, slinging his arms and stomping his feet, trying to keep the circulation going. It had begun to snow. The flakes were blinding me. I could hardly see the mules ahead. I loose-hooked my checkreins and set the brake on a notch that would allow the wheels to barely turn, holding the wagon back off the mules. I was going to let them have their head.

After doing this, I crawled to the rear of the wagon and eased myself to the ground. I started stomping my feet and slinging my arms every which way. My teeth were sounding like a jack hammer, they were chattering so.

I was telling Artie all this while I was having some hamburgers and hot black coffee in the little restaurant.

You have often heard older people say that when young boys start to drink coffee it will stunt their growth. Well, that's not true. I

41

started drinking it on my first trip over the mountain and I grew up to over six feet tall.

While sitting there, talking, Artie said she and Amos wanted to thank me for what I had done. She had spent $142 for the gifts and wanted me to have what was left. I told her to keep it, that I wanted her to get something she needed, or spend it any way she pleased and to not mention it anymore. She did keep it.

SIX

TIMES WERE GETTING WORSE every day. People that had farms raised a lot of food, canning it and drying some, dry curing their pork, and keeping a few milk cows. They were really lucky.

The next morning I was having my wagon loaded at the wholesale. As I stood there on the loading dock, a large group of people came rushing down the street. They started milling and crowding at the entrance of the county maintenance building directly across the street from where I was standing. Each man was trying to be the first one through the door.

A big man wearing a dark blue suit came out the door, waving a piece of yellow paper, and calling to the crowd to quiet down. He had something he wanted to read to them. It was a telegram from Washington.

After he told them who he was, they all quieted down. The telegram stated that he, Mr. T.R. Brockland, was to have the assistance of the sheriff's office and certified deputy clerks from the county clerk's office to set up a suitable system to register each and every person in Harlan County that met the requirements and needed assistance for food. Signed by the President of these United States of America.

He further said the registering system would start tomorrow morning and to please pass the word throughout the area where they lived. He said those whose last name began in the first half of the alphabet would sign up the first day, the others the next day. He stated that he was wiring for a shipment of commodities immediately. The crowd yelled and applauded him and went back up the street, slapping each other on the back and wondering what kind of food the government would give them.

The registering of the people was over by Friday, and people were coming into town by the hundreds. Some had no transportation and had to walk as much as twenty miles. They were coming to try to get food for their families, for they were near starving.

The big coal companies, before they closed their mines, were paying fifteen cents a ton for loading coal. The coal miner had to buy from the company the explosives to blast the coal loose. In a hard day's work back under the mountain each miner would load as much as ten tons of coal. They would rush to the company store to line up at the paycheck office. The pay they got would be scrip, which meant it was a company check that was acceptable only at the company's own store. With this kind of system the entire county was declared in a state of poverty.

Sometime the following Tuesday night the L. & N. Railroad sidetracked seven boxcars near the county maintenance building. County employees began unloading and sorting the foods. Some of the foods that came off the boxcars were cheese, large cans of pork or stringy beef, big slabs of salt bacon, cans of lard, flour, dried milk, meal, beans, and many more items. By day's end, thousands of families were sitting down to a good supper.

Some families were given grapefruits. Thinking they were oranges, a lot of people didn't know how to eat them. I heard of some baking them and some grinding them and then boiling them, mixing flour in to cause it to thicken and then serving it as a dessert. The mountain people were ignorant of a lot of foreign and southern food.

Some of the mine owners offered ten cents a ton to the miners if they would give up getting relief food from the government and report to the mines. None of the miners reported. They were eating good now, but they didn't have any money. If they stopped getting relief and went back to the mines, they wouldn't have any money and they sure couldn't feed their families on ten cents a ton. It was this simple.

The weather was beginning to warm up now. The rivers and streams had thawed. It was about the middle of April. The people that owned bottomland were plowing and some were clearing hillsides of brush thickets, making space to plant all sorts of vegetables. The rivers and larger streams were filled with fish. Big patches of mountain laurel and dogwood were in full bloom and covered the mountainsides and ridges.

I had fared pretty good through the winter. My team of big black mules were slick fat. Uncle John had tended them good. When some days I didn't go to the barn, he would give them tender loving care and wouldn't take any pay. He said, "I just naturally love to take care of such fine animals." I could not argue with him about that.

I got enough work during the winter to keep all my bills paid. I'd make sometimes three trips a month over the mountains to the school. My big blacks were about the only team around that could pull a wagon loaded usually with two to three tons of food supplies. On heavier loads I'd sometimes hire a span of mules or horses.

I had gotten my brother-in-law to scotch for me, since JoJo had gone to work for the county road gang. He often said, "If I could get a job where I could save enough money, I'd buy a team of mules just like yours." He might start saving, now he was making more than I paid him.

Amos had worked in the coal mines since he was twelve years old and didn't have a thing to show for it except a wife and three rooms of furniture, and it not paid for. But that shouldn't have been his fault. The big coal mine owners would work men till they dropped over, paying them as little as they could get by with.

On one of the trips over the mountain, Amos told me Artie had made three payments on their furniture with the money I gave her for Christmas. He said, "By the food relief I'm getting and the pay you give me, Artie and I are doing all right."

It was now the last of May and the government relief was still going on. All the loaded coal cars had been taken to the northern factories and were strung out on the sidetracks, sitting there empty.

The mine owners had organized themselves, and their organization was named the Harlan County Coal Operators' Association. This body of men was the cause of many murders and beatings. They sent delegates to Frankfort, the state capitol, with great sums of money to gain favors from the governor and the other state officials.

The sheriff had lost his bid for reelection, and the H.C.C.O.A. (the mine owners) had selected a man of their own choice to run for sheriff. After this man's election, he hired every criminal he could find in surrounding counties and a lot in our own county. He put badges on their shirts and big guns on their hips. These men would get a few days of briefing and then, in pairs, would be sent to coal camps to beat and pistol-whip miners if they refused to work in the mines. The non-working miners started arming themselves after finding their kin and friends murdered and lying in ditches.

The deputies were hired by the hundreds by the new sheriff. Then the mine owners would move them into a nice big company house and give them a new fast car. They would drive their shiny new car through the coal camps with blinkers on and the siren screaming, up to some non-working miner's house. Leaving the blinkers flashing, they would jump from the car, one carrying an automatic shotgun, the other with a long padded billy-club loaded with lead dangling on his side.

One would dash to the rear of the house. The other, rushing to the front, would crash the flimsy door in. They would demand, from a scared and terrified woman, "Where is that God-damn Russian Red son-of-a bitch?" The woman would start pleading for them to not hurt her husband, that she would get him to go back to work in the mines, or that they would leave the camp.

The other camp boss would be guarding the rear of the house. If the husband or father should attempt to escape through the rear he would be blasted with shots from the guard's shotgun. The murdering thug would then call to his partner that he had got the thieving bastard. The mine guards would leave the body lying where it fell.

The wife, with a small child in her arms, would be kneeling by her husband's body, sobbing and praying to the Lord to stop the killings the mine owners were ordering. Wives of other miners who were working would come running and together they'd drag the body in the house. The women would clean and dress the corpse for burial. The mine owners would send a cheap casket to the house, and the grieving family and friends would carry the body up on the hillside for burial.

The mine owners, after getting the reports from their hired thugs, would report to the sheriff's office that a man had been killed by mistake. They would say that they had thought someone was trying to break into one of the employees' homes and then trying to escape, so they mistakenly shot and killed him. That and other similar reports were put on file and probably are there yet.

The delegates the mine owners had sent to Frankfort stayed informed of all the actions the protective deputy sheriffs were taking to keep the willing miners (those who were working) from being beaten and murdered by roving bands of United Mine Workers that were scattered throughout the mountains. They were armed with high-powered rifles furnished to them by union officials in Washington, D.C. When the mine owners began presenting these facts to the governor, things began to happen.

The Kentucky State Military Office was directed to send fifty units of cavalry, with their mounts, to Harlan County. They were to report to the sheriff and work under his direction to bring a halt to the rampaging United Mine Workers of America, to keep them from slaughtering good, honest, hard-working miners that were trying to make a living mining coal. They were also to give assistance to the deputy sheriffs that were being ambushed and beaten by the roving mobs of United Mine Workers.

People said the governor was a big stockholder in some of the coal companies.

The long train pulled into Harlan bringing help to stop the killings and beatings that were happening every day. The sheriff, with personal body guards, was there to greet them. After unloading all the horses and ammunition, the cavalry made camp and set up headquarters in a big field that was across the tracks from the H.T. Hackney Wholesale. All the town people swarmed around, watching and asking each other what was happening. Some thought they were preparing for a full-scale war.

All the enlisted military men were going about their duties with side arms and rifles slung over their shoulders and steel helmets on their heads. It sure was a scary looking time.

Several women were there that had lost their husbands to the brutal, death-dealing deputies. They were crying and telling the people to arm themselves and go home, lock their doors, and shoot any of the bastards that came near their homes.

It was now the last of May. The governor of Kentucky got the federal government to stop shipping food to the striking miners. When this happened everybody thought the miners would end their strike and return to the mines. The mine owners were offering to raise their pay from seventeen cents a ton to twenty-six cents a ton, but the workers would have to walk or crawl to and from their working places in the mine.

Some of the striking miners returned. They soon found the offer had been made only to get them to move into the coal camps. They would then be forced to work, sometimes with beatings and threats of what would happen to them and their kin if they failed to report for work. These beatings and threats came from the mine protection thugs. The military men paraded through the coal camps in full combat uniform, insulting young girls and wives of men that were underground loading coal.

The military men would tell the younger girls that if they refused, or reported the men to their commanding officer, they would have the deputies to take their fathers or husbands for a ride over the mountain on a one-way trip.

The young girls and married women would agree to the demands. After this started, some of the girls and women would tell their kin what had happened. The fathers and husbands would get word to the roving groups of United Mine Workers, explaining that they were being forced to work and about their daughters and wives being forced to submit to the military men.

The roving men, working in unison with their groups, would rendezvous and plot their retaliations on the thugs and military men.

At one place, a group of roving men had barricaded themselves on a rocky point that extended all the way down to the road. This caused the road to have a sharp curve. Another group positioned themselves the same way just across the creek, facing the curve.

A big military truck came slowly around the curve. A small car in front had three company protectors in it. Rifles started firing from both sides and the rear. Some of the rovers were firing from the front. Fourteen military men and three thugs were riddled with bullets. The rovers dashed gas on the vehicles. Then they set the car and truck aflame and took to the hills.

When the news of this reached the town of Harlan, the sheriff and the commanding officer declared the entire county to be under martial law. This was the day the United Mine Workers' Union shipped in food for the striking men.

When two or more men gathered, the military men would scatter them with threats, shoving, pushing, and sometimes cracking them over their shoulders with their rifles. The union food was being doled out to the waiting lines of eager men that probably hadn't had a good meal since the government stopped sending food in to feed them.

It was now July 9. Tomorrow I would be fourteen years old. My height was six feet. I weighed 132 pounds. All bone and muscle. I was my own man, or that's the way I thought of myself.

All this trouble of people being killed, their women being raped, their homes being dynamited, burned, and shot into, was doing something to me at night. As I lay in bed trying to go to sleep, and sleep not coming to my eyes, I would just stare at the ceiling. I could see men lying in ditches with the whole tops of their heads shot off. Men floating down Martin's Fork, bloated beyond recognition. I could see deputies rolling bodies of striking miners over the edges of the road, watching them roll and slide into deep, dark wooded ravines.

I laid there and decided to myself that never would I become a coal miner and chance myself to the treatment and trouble that goes with it. I lay there, clenching my fists, straining every muscle within me.

I had seen men who were being taken to jail shot by deputies for jerking loose and running. They ran because they feared the jail, knowing that when they got there the jailer would allow the deputies to enter the cell and beat them with leaded rubber hoses, trying to make them confess to some killing or tell of plans the union was plotting, until the deputies had tired themselves. When a victim became unconscious or died, the deputies would report to the county judge that the man had died from a heart attack. These things happened every day the miners were on strike.

I woke the next morning ready to look the world in the eye, it being the day I became fourteen years old. Amos was working with me yet. We did a lot of garden plowing for the town people and hauling building materials from the depot to the new hotel going up, and making regular trips across Pine Mountain to the school.

Amos had stopped getting government food shortly after he started working with me. The owner of the house Artie and Amos lived in built another room onto the house and gave them an old iron bed stand. When the room was finished Artie asked me to come and live with her and Amos. I hated to leave Mrs. Walters. She looked after me more than she did her own. But Artie was my sister and we loved each other very much.

I gave Artie some money to buy a cotton mattress to put on the iron bed. She had been making quilts and had several completed. Mom had given her an old ticking of goose feathers to sleep under on cold nights. Artie fixed the new room up real nice. She put a wall oil lamp by the bed and a small table with a cane-bottom chair, and placed a large hook rug by the side of the bed.

I brought my clothes from Mrs. Walters'. The next evening, while Artie was straightening and hanging my clothes, Amos and I were eating supper. She had cooked a big fat hen and made a pot of dumplings and all the trimmings that go with it.

The big factories and steel mills in the northern cities were demanding coal to feed their huge furnaces. The automobile factories were building bigger plants. The town paper, the *Harlan Daily Enter-*

prise, had the front page covered with news about the fast way things were sprouting up all over the country. Work up north was really booming.

The mine owners in Harlan were thinking they were getting the short end of all this sudden growth in business. They called for a meeting with the officials of the U.M.W. of A. to discuss a contract with them. The owners fired all their thugs and the state military moved out.

The union was still sending plenty of food into Harlan and they stood a pat hand for a good contract. The mine owners were becoming humble to the union's stiff plan for contracts. Some of the bigger companies wanted a sweetheart contract and wanted the union to draw up harder contracts for the smaller companies. But the union didn't do business like that. Their offer was the same to each and every coal company in Harlan County. After all the haggling and cursing was done, each mine owner signed the agreement to accept the union's contract.

This news spread throughout the county fast. The union told the miners to report to the mines where they were working when the strike started. They would be put to work doing the same job they were doing before they struck.

This was the greatest thing that ever happened, bringing all of Harlan County's mine owners under union ruling.

SEVEN

THINGS SURE went to popping soon. Money began flowing from the many coal camps into town. Merchants started stocking their shelves with all kinds of pretty clothes. The big hotel was completed. A big lumber company put in a large mill that turned out finished smooth lumber. A new wholesale opened up. Hundreds of things were happening to Harlan. Ben Howard, my street boss, got a contract to finish the streets all over town. Things were booming.

I stayed with Artie the rest of the summer. Amos and me were doing a lot of heavy hauling all over town. I didn't work for Ben anymore until late fall.

The trips over the mountain had slowed down. The Pine Mountain School students worked in fields, raising all the vegetables they needed and feed for all their milk cows and for fattening hogs. They kept two big barns filled with chickens, getting all the eggs and poultry meat they needed. A load of other supplies every now and then was all they needed until winter set in.

The coal miners, after gaining their contract with mine operators, were enjoying their victory. Their pay had been raised greatly. A lot of them would come to town driving new cars and wearing pretty new clothes.

It just didn't seem like this was the same town. A few short months earlier it had been bathed in blood and all the streets in town and the coal camps were filled with gun thugs and mounted state military people who paraded around killing, raping, and taking anything they wanted that was of any value from the striking miners.

This Sunday morning, on a chilly October day, white clouds were floating overhead. Silvery rays of a bright sun shining on them met me as I stood there on the porch waiting for Amos to say bye to Artie and tell her we would be back by dinner time. He asked her to fix a good Sunday dinner, for there was going to be company to feed.

As we trudged through the muddy streets on our way through town, we were on our way to the livery stable to patch up some worn parts of my harness and grease the spinnels of the wagon. When we got there Uncle John was brushing the big blacks and talking to them like they were understanding everything he was saying. We joshed him about it and had a good laugh. He sure liked them big mules. We put the saddles on the mules to ride back across town. The mules were shining like black velvet. The sun had pushed the clouds away and it was the brightest day I ever remember.

As we rode through town, people stood in front of stores and up and down the boarded walks watching us as we cantered past them, the big saddles shining and the large cantlehorns gleaming. A lot of bright silvery brads decorated the stirrup boots and the large side flaps. We were getting a lot of attention as we rode by.

When we neared home, Amos told me that Mom and Dad and Jim would be there for dinner. I don't know why he didn't want me to know before. He knew why I was away from home, and how they had hated me when I left. Since Dad had sold all his work stock to the sawmill company and gone back to farming, he didn't seem like the same man. When I would see him in town he seemed to want to talk to me a lot. He just acted like nothing had ever happened between us.

We turned the big black mules loose in Artie's garden lot, laid our saddles on the porch, and went in the house. Mom, Dad, and Jim were sitting by the fire. Artie was tending her cooking.

Jim got up, came over and put an arm around my shoulder, patting me on the back and wanting to know how I and my team were doing. He started in telling me about working on a coal tipple. "I'm getting paid four dollars and ten cents for just working eight hours. Also, I have a girlfriend." While he was telling me about her, his face lit up like an electric light bulb. She was the prettiest girl he ever knew and she loved him and they were getting married.

Mom spoke to me about how tall I was getting and said, "You ought to come back home and I'll put some meat on them bones." She felt my shoulder and said, "You're nothing but skin and bones."

I said, "There has to be some muscle underneath, for I have been doing a lot of work."

Mom went to the kitchen to help Artie set up dinner. Dad wanted to know if I was planning on hauling to the school the rest of the winter. I told him I hadn't plumb made up my mind about it yet.

Last winter had been awful bad and I had thought I'd freeze a few times. It showed up on my mules that they were being overworked. Some of the loads should have had a span of Morgans up front.

Dad said, "Let's go look at your mules while the women are fixing dinner."

Jim said, "I believe I'll go with you."

Amos, coming in from the kitchen, said, "I've become a mule lover and I would like to go, too."

We walked over to the garden fence. The mules were at the other side of the lot, munching around old dead weeds, finding a few tender bites down close to the ground. I called them to me. As the mules came up, trotting and slinging their heads, Dad said, "Jim, that sure is a fine looking pair of mules."

I reached over the fence, rubbing their noses and heads. They expected to be rubbed and petted when they weren't harnessed, but when they were harnessed they knew the petting was over.

Dad said to me, "I'd like to talk to you about something after we eat dinner."

Artie had cooked a real good dinner. Mom and her had it spread out on the table, with plenty more in the pots setting on the back of the stove. They had big pones of cornbread and hot biscuits setting in the warming closet.

Artie and Amos had gone into town the evening before to buy the next week's groceries. They had a few extra dollars to spend and they bought a lot of good things they knew Mom and Dad liked. I better not start telling what she had fixed for dinner. If I did, I'd have to get up and feed my hungry pains.

After dinner was over we all sat around the table. Just about everything you could think of was talked about. Mom was saying how glad she was that none of her kin had been hurt or killed in the coal strike, and how fast the town was growing. With all the money being spread about town, you'd think someone in Harlan had a money making machine.

Mom and Dad were talking like I was somebody else, not the one they had run off from home. As they sat there, talking, laughing, and drinking coffee, I went into something like a trance. Things kept flashing through my head about the past. I just couldn't believe it was me they were talking to.

Artie started clearing the table and Mom was covering the pots with lids and placing them on the far back of the stove to keep the food warm for a late supper. Dad asked me to come with him, he wanted to look at the mules again. Jim and Amos wanted to play some kind of a card game.

Dad and I walked out to the garden lot. The big mules came over to us for some more nose rubbing.

Dad said, "I have a good job lined up for you. If you are interested in it, I will help you get it." He said, "You have such a good team of mules and a heavy strong wagon that you could handle it. The company Jim works for wants to hire a big team to do the company hauling." I would be delivering coal from the tipple to the miners' homes and hauling mine supplies from the depot and loads of store goods for the wholesales to their store. The pay would be a lot better than I was making now.

It sounded good. I had been making decisions on doing hauling jobs for a good while now, and I made a fair price to anybody I was working for. I mulled it around in my mind for a few minutes, while Dad was rubbing one of the big blacks on the nose. After wrestling it around for a while, I started to pace back and forth to the gate and commenced to think about the others.

My brothers and sisters, I missed them awfully. Sometimes I'd see one or two together in town. They'd bring baskets of eggs and large molds of fresh churned butter to trade for some store-bought foodstuff. We'd sometimes go to the little hamburger restaurant and I'd buy us something to eat. They'd want to know why I stayed away from home all the time, and why wouldn't Mom and Dad let them come and see me when they came to town. I would make all kinds of excuses, but never did I tell them the truth about it.

Dad was still petting and rubbing the big blacks, as I turned to him to give an answer. I told him, "I think I'll take the offer, if they'll let me start on the fifteenth of next month." I had promised Ben that I would use the slip scrapers to open and drain all the ditches on the streets that were ready to be paved. The cold weather had come early, before he could pave them. I had two or more trips to make to the school, too, then I would hire to them.

Dad thought that would be all right. He looked pleased about it. Then he asked if I wanted to come back home.

I told him what Mom had started to tell me the night he went after Amos. He said he had been drinking a lot that day and hardly knew what he was saying. He said he knew he put more dependence in Jim, but him being older, he felt he was letting him do the more responsible work and me the lighter part. He said, "Jim getting married will make it mighty hard on me." The other boys were too small to be any kind of help and he needed me to be around to help keep the farming going when I wasn't doing any hauling for the coal company.

He said that I could keep my mules in a big company barn they had built at the foot of the mountain where you turn up the hill to go home, and I could use it for free. It had a big boarded fence around it and the stream ran right through the middle of it. There were ten stalls and a hay loft overhead, already filled with good bales of hay, and about fifty 100-pound sacks of feed in the grain room. Dad said that I could use all the hay and feed that was stored at the barn. The company had gotten rid of all their horses and small mules. I wouldn't have to pay a cent for it.

He went on, telling me a pretty tale of how everything would be if I would come back home.

Did you ever have a feeling you were being built up by someone else's promises, only to have them later to come back and knock the props from under you? Well, that was what was happening to me now.

Dad said, "I would like to ride with you in the wagon when you would be hauling coal and mining supplies. I could be a lot of help loading and unloading heavy boxes, crates, and barrels of mining machinery oil."

Something kept bearing on me that this was too much to be true.

Amos and I were at the livery stable the next morning around four o'clock. We harnessed the big blacks and geared them to the wagon, getting ready to drive across town to the H.T. Hackney Wholesale.

The load I was to take across the mountain was stashed in a pick-up locker at the end of the loading dock. It was beginning to get daylight when we finished loading. We wanted to make it about halfway up the mountain by nightfall. I didn't have a very heavy load, mostly early Christmas stuff and trimmings for Thanksgiving.

All the snow had melted and the road was awfully muddy. We made camp at a little flattened bank on top of a steep climb and fared kindly well through the night. We made it to the school the next day, arriving just at dark. A bunch of students swarmed around the wagon and offered to unload while Amos and I tended the big mules. The cook fixed us a bite to eat and then bedded us in a little room off of the cook's cabin. The cook said, "I will have you a good breakfast as early as you want it." I told him I'd like to leave at the crack of dawn, that I was to pick up a load of stuff for Mr. Ford.

We stayed the next night at a big new log house way back up on the side of Kentucky Ridge. We had arrived at good dark. The next morning my wagon was loaded and the big blacks were standing there hitched and ready to go.

There's something about this breed of mountain people. They think if they don't do something for you, like having my mules harnessed and hitched and the wagon loaded, you'd think they were unfriendly.

We had no trouble at all coming back across. We pulled our wagon under Mr. Roark's barn shed, tended the mules, and took off for the house. It was now pitch dark. Mrs. Roark had heard us drive up and was getting us something to eat. While we were eating, Mr. and Mrs. Roark were talking a mile a minute, wanting to know all about the fast way Harlan was growing, and how everybody in town was.

I was so hungry, I let Amos do the answering and I kept on eating. After we ate, Mrs. Roark and her son Todd wanted to sing a few old mountain ballads, with Mr. Roark and the other sons pitching in with their music. This went on till I got sleepy and went to bed.

When we got back to Harlan we drove up to Mr. Ford's cellar door and started carrying furs, cow hides, and all the other stuff that was the rest of the load. I had brought him 550 gallons of corn liquor. Mr. Ford said this was supposed to be the best liquor he had ever gotten from across the mountain. He asked me to drop off two jugs at the former sheriff's house and tell him to have a good Christmas.

After delivering the two jugs, I dropped Amos off at his house and drove over to Ben's office. He lined me up on the work he wanted done. It would take me ten days to do all the ditching and draining. I still had plenty of time to drive to the coal company's office and ask about the job Dad was telling me about. The pay I was to get amounted to a lot more than I had been making. I asked about the hay and feed that was at the barn.

About that time the superintendent came in the office and wanted to know who owned that team of big black mules. I told him I did. He looked me up and down for a minute, me standing there like a shike poke, tall, skinny, and bony. I told him who my Dad was and he said, "You sure don't look like your dad. I was just talking with him a week or so back, offered him a good job if he could find a good strong team of mules."

I then told him why I was there. We left the office for him to look at the big blacks. He checked every bolt and board on my wagon. Then, walking from one mule to the other, patting and rubbing their nose, he looked to me and said, "You're just a kid. How come you've got such a fine team of mules and your dad don't own any?"

After the way he looked at me and told me I didn't look like Dad, I thought I'd better not do any explaining to him. It wasn't the first time I had been told I most likely was a stray colt.

I asked him if he wanted to hire me and my team or not. I told him that I hadn't come to see him about running down blood lines. I started climbing up to the seat. He said, "Hold on there a minute, let's do some talking. I didn't aim to insult you. I just thought it odd, you being so young and owning an outfit like this."

I told him I didn't own an outfit, that I owned the best damn team of mules and one of the strongest and best cared for wagons in the whole damn state of Kentucky. I picked up my check lines and called out to the lead mule to gee. (Gee means turn to the right; haw means go left.) He grabbed the bridle of the lead mule and stopped him from geeing.

The superintendent said, "Man, you sure got some pepper in you. I'd be proud to be your friend and I sure as hell want you to work. Now get down off that wagon and let's go in the store and get acquainted. I sure like to meet somebody that's got some spunk." That sorta cooled me off a mite, when he talked to me like that. I climbed off the wagon and walked into the company store with him.

The store manager was behind a long counter, filling an order for the big boarding house. He had half the counter covered. All kinds of canned foods, big paper-wrapped packs of fresh meats, flour, apples, and just about anything you could think of to eat was piled on that counter.

Mr. Martin (I later learned his first name was Bill) came to us and the superintendent said, "Mr. Martin, I'd like you to know my friend and the owner of the finest looking team and wagon that's in the whole state of Kentucky." He looked to me and asked, "What's your name?"

I told him my name was Green, but everybody called me Red. I took my canvas cap off and my hair showed bright red, standing underneath the light.

Mr. Martin said, "I sure can see why they call you Red."

The superintendent said, "I better introduce myself. My name is Bassham, Theodore Pearl Bassham, but the miners that don't like me call me the Pearly Bastard, and my friends call me Pearl." He said he would like me to drop the Mr. and call him Pearl. He told Mr. Martin what duties I would be doing as of in the morning.

Mr. Martin said, "I wished it was now." He was having to tote this whole order of food to the boarding house up on top of the ridge overlooking the coal camp. My wagon was sitting out front of the office so I offered to haul them up there so I could have a sky view of all the coal camp. Mr. Bassham said, "That would be fine, and I would like to ride with you."

We loaded the groceries and started going up. The hill was terribly steep. The wagon alone would have been a large load for an ordinary team, but them big blacks topped it with ease. Mr. Bassham told me after we got back off the hill that he liked the way my mules responded to each command I gave them, and he was very happy to have me and the team in his charge.

I asked him about the feed and hay at the barn, if I could use it. "Sure, go ahead, but we will have to have at least half our cost from your pay." I agreed that was fair.

I left my wagon at the front of the store. I rode one mule and led the other to the barn. This was a much warmer place than the livery stable. It had big roomy stalls and a hay rack that would hold a whole bale of hay, with a big feed box and a block of salt for the mules to lick on.

Jim had gotten married while I was making my last trip over the mountain, and was now not working. I reckoned that young married couples don't have time to work. They got so many other things to do that they just lay work aside until they catch up on other things. Anyhow, he lost his job by missing too many days' work.

Dad had been riding around with me, admiring the work I was doing. Sometimes he would drive to town to pick up some mining supplies or take a load of groceries to the boarding house, leaving me at the store to loaf a while. He sure was treating me kindly. Every evening he'd try to get me to go home with him. He said, "The kids are wanting you bad." But I couldn't bring myself to do it.

I was still staying with Artie. Amos had gotten a job from Bassham, in the mines, and was doing just fine. Artie was working three or four days a week doing housecleaning for some of the bigwigs in town, and I began to feel like I was too much extra trouble for

Artie to have around. She kept all my clothes washed and ironed and put in order in my room. I always had me a good hot supper ready to sit down to. After I'd had my supper she'd have a big wash tub half full of good warm water over near the cookstove, and a clean change of clothes laid neatly in a chair. Sometimes she'd complain about me coming in with so much coal black on me, or ask me why I hadn't stomped the mud off my boots, and why couldn't I be there when she and Amos sat down to eat. She said, "Since I started working in town, it looks like you and Amos are trying to see how much more work I will have to do at home."

I couldn't hardly believe that was Artie talking. She had always been so kind and meek towards me and Amos. She was always going behind us, picking up our discarded dirty clothes, seeing to us having clean beds, with big fluffed-up feather pillows and big thick comforters laying folded across the foot of the bed to pull up over us in the early morning hours after the fire had died out and the house started getting cold.

I was sitting there staring, not seeing anything, just letting one thing and another run through my mind. I was a grown man, nearly, and here I was making like this was my own house and home. Thinking because I laid a goodly sum of money on the table each week, that it gave me the privilege to do so.

Artie turned to me, and asked, "What are you staring at?" She came over and sat down. We sat there looking at each other. Each one wanted to say something but didn't know how to begin, afraid it might not come out the way we meant it to. Finally I broke out of my trance and told her I had been thinking of going back home. I told her about Dad asking me so many times and telling me how our brothers and sisters missed me and that it was near Christmas and he would like for me to be there.

Artie said she thought that I should, but I was still welcomed to stay there as long as I wanted to. She said that if I did go back, the first time they started in on me, for me to come right back there.

I sat there a long time after she had cleared the table and washed the dishes. Her and Amos had gone to bed hours ago. I just sat there thinking and remembering all the good things that ever happened to me, and then the bitter thought of never having heard a kind word or feeling an affectionate touch from my mother or father. The only kindness I can ever remember came from Artie. The thoughts of the night Mom laid a bundle of my clothes at my feet kept coming before me.

The next morning, I crammed some of my clothes in an old canvas bag and went to work. I put the bag in my possible box, then headed to the barn. Jim and Dad had the mules harnessed and were coming through the gate, leading them.

Dad said, "I thought Jim ought to help you on the wagon. It's too hard for you to keep up all the hauling done with no more help than I have been giving." He said, "You are supposed to deliver ten loads of coal, plus all the other hauling. That's just too much for you to tackle by yourself." I was beginning to think he was about to treat me as their equal.

Jim and I got a lot of work done that day, but he talked about how great it was to be married and how good and warm it was to crawl in bed to a warm, loving, and willing wife. He kept going on like this all day.

Dad had hung around the company store all day, swapping yarns and tales with the miners who worked on the night shift. It had been a cold day. Jim and I had worked hard since daybreak and got the hauling caught up, but tomorrow I would probably have more to do than I got done today. With all the snowing and freezing, and then the melting on a sunny day causing big sloppy mud holes all through the camp, it was hard for the big black mules to pull a loaded wagon through it.

Dad stood inside the store, watching through the window for Jim and me to come by the store so he could ride with us to the barn. When he saw us coming he came toward us, pulling his coat collar up around his neck and carrying a small paper bag filled with peppermint stick candy. He climbed up into the wagon and offered us some of it. I told him I couldn't get my mouth opened wide enough to eat it without breaking my jaws.

We made our way through the muddy roads and creek to the barn. Before we got there one of the worst snow blizzards I ever saw was moving in. Jim and I were already about froze. The wind came, facing us, with great sheets of big flakes of snow. The wind was howling through the trees and over the mules and wagon. Every now and then you could hear a limb crack from a tree and then see it come sailing through the air. Some fell around and on the mules, causing them to jump and jerk the wagon around till we could hardly stay in it.

We drove into the hallway of the barn and closed the big doors. I fumbled around and got two lanterns lit. The dim light shining on the mules made them look as if they were covered with a white sheet. We got some old feed sacks and started wiping and brushing the snow and ice off them. We got them unharnessed and dried them off good. Then we put plenty of feed and hay in for them.

It sure was a bad storm. The snow was blowing through some of the cracks of the barn and the wind was whistling like a big band tuning their horns. We climbed up in the loft and crawled deep in the hay to wait out the storm.

After lying there in the hay, I started dozing. When I woke up, the wind had quieted and I was good and warm. I crept out from the hay. Jim and Dad had fared good where they had slept. The hay had dried all the dampness from our clothes, but the cold was chilling us to the bone.

It was getting a little light outside. We climbed down from the loft and in the middle of a big stall we gathered some sawed-off ends of boards and started a small fire. I always kept my coffee pot and some coffee in my possible box. I got it out and melted snow to make coffee. By then, it was good daylight.

I opened the big door and went out to see about the froze-up creek. The mules hadn't gotten to drink last night. It looked like the creek was froze solid. I got my ice axe from the wagon and started chopping through a deep part of the creek. It was about eight or ten inches thick. Jim and I led the big blacks down to drink. When they got out of the warm barn they started to humping up and drawed their tails down real tight to cover the most exposed parts of their bodies from the freezing air.

I knew the mines would not work today. Snow had drifted in some places over four feet. It would take all the companies' outside workers all day to clear the tracks and thaw out the rail switches.

The big blacks drank till I thought they were going to burst. They had stomped and snorted around all night, pawing and rubbing their necks and shoulders and hips against their scratch poles. I gave them enough grain to eat for the rest of the day, and threw each one a bale of hay and propped their doors back so they could have their freedom in the barn lot to get a drink.

I then buttoned my coat up tight, pulled my sock cap down over my ears, and tied my overall legs tight around my ankles. I covered my boots real heavy with axle grease to keep them from soaking in the dampness. I climbed up on the wagon and got my canvas bag and strapped it to my back. Jim wanted to know what I had in my bag. He didn't know Dad had asked me to come back home.

We took off up the mountain trail, making our way through big drifts, having to grab hold of tree limbs and branches to pull ourselves along. Sometimes Jim and I would help Dad through steep climbs and snow banks all along the trail. It was close to four miles back up on the mountain to the house, but after you got there, you would envy Dad. He had everything the flatland people had and a lot more. He had all things that made mountain living a comfort.

EIGHT

IT TOOK OVER two hours of hard climbing before we reached the house. Mom saw us coming, fighting our way along the trail. By the time we got there she was putting food on the table, and a big coffee pot was steaming.

Mom went to Dad and gave him a pat or two on the arm. She laid a hand on Jim's shoulders and started asking them a lot of questions. Finally she looked at me and asked if I had come back to stay. This was the first time I had been back on the mountain since she had put my bag of clothes at my feet. I told her that Dad had been asking me to come back for over a month.

Lilian, Jim's wife, came into the kitchen and started kissing and hugging him, crying and slobbering all over him. The other children were crowding around, glimpsing our condition and asking all sorts of questions, like "Why didn't you come home last night?"

Lilian and Mom started pouring coffee, taking hot biscuits from the oven. All the food looked good, and I was hungry, but somehow I knew I wasn't going to enjoy it. It had been almost two years since I had sat at this table, and I had done a lot of growing up in this time. I knew how to work out nearly any kind of problem that might come before me. But coming back home (or can I call it home?) was a problem that had me thinking.

I knew I would always be treated like one that didn't belong there. Dad and Jim were cramming their food in like they were starved. I took a sip or two of coffee. Mom said, "You'd better eat something or you'll get sick, and Artie ain't here to doctor you."

Right then I was wishing I was at Artie's or Mrs. Walters'. Lilian came and sat beside me. She put an egg and a slice of ham on my plate and a buttered biscuit and told me to eat it. I hadn't ever spoken to her before and these were the first words she ever said to me. I had seen her a few times around town but didn't know who she was. Taking her advice, I ate what she put on my plate.

I was getting thawed by now, and asked Lilian if she knew where I could put my bag of clothes. Mom told her I could sleep with the other boys. She said, "I'll fix him a bed in the other corner, across from theirs."

I just sat around the fire till in the evening, talking with my two younger brothers, William and Dave, answering their questions the best I could.

I had quite a bit of money stowed with my bag of clothes. I asked Mom if I could give it to her. She said, "I will look after it for you the best I can."

I counted out over $300 and handed it to her. My baby brothers said, "That must be all the money there is in the world!"

I told Mom the money was for her, that she could spend it for Christmas, any way she wanted to. Mom kindly showed a little more interest in me after that. She even asked me if I would like to have her bake a big apple cobbler for supper and fry some chicken. That sure did shake me up. Never before in my life could I remember her asking me if I wanted anything special to eat or hearing her speak to me in such a kind voice.

Mom and the girls went to the kitchen to prepare supper. Each one was trying to do more than the other one to help. Mom was fixing the apples, with three or four different kinds of mountain spices. Narciss, with Lilian helping, was getting the chicken ready to fry. The other girls were wiping the table clean and setting it up with the dishes I'd got Artie to get for Mom last Christmas. I could hear the girls talking to Mom. They were trying to talk all at the same time, telling her what they wanted for Christmas.

I was thinking about my big blacks. I had left them well cared for. They had plenty of hay and enough grain to do them till Sunday. I had chopped a big hole in the ice and I knew they'd keep it open with their forefeet, pawing it with their iron shoes to get to the water.

After a while Lilian called for everybody to come to supper. The family took their regular places at the table and sat down. Mom was at the stove, stirring a big iron skillet of milk gravy. She said, "Sit in my place, I will tend the table while we eat." This kind of treatment I couldn't hardly believe.

After supper was over, Jim and I tended all the stock and milked the cows. Then we rolled a big back log in the fireplace, got the fire relit, and all the family sat around it baking their shins and talking about Christmas and how cold it was. I was being included in nearly all the things that were talked about. The room was lit up good from the big fireplace and everybody seemed comfortable just setting there, enjoying the warmth.

Lilian asked if anybody wanted to bake some dried corn and potatoes in the ashes. Everybody said, "That would be fun." Now, the way you roast dried corn is to lay the ear near the red hot ashes and turn it often to let it brown. Then you put a smearing of butter on to melt through the grains, salt lightly, and hope you don't break a tooth when you eat it. We enjoyed the corn and baked potatoes till time to go to bed.

Mom had fixed me a good bed. It had big springy corn shuck ticking on the bottom and a thick feather ticking on top of it. She had put two of her best quilts on for the covers. After being nearly froze the night before, getting to sleep in this warm bed is just something I can't describe to you, the comfort I got from laying there.

As I laid there, letting my thoughts wander back to sleepless nights of cold camping on trips across the mountain and restless nights at Mrs. Walters' and Artie's, I got to wondering if the way I was growing into a man was the way the Lord meant it to be. I closed my eyes and thought a silent prayer of thanks for all the good things he had given me and for helping me over the rough places, to where I was now.

When I woke up the next morning, I went to the front porch and looked up to the sky. Not a cloud could I see. The sun was shining on the snow. It sparkled like millions and millions of diamonds and rubies reflecting from the sun.

Dad and Jim were clearing the snow from around the barn doors and corncribs and making paths to the milking sheds. Mom and all the others were in the kitchen cooking breakfast. As I entered the kitchen, Mom asked me if I had slept good and if I wanted a cup of coffee.

This was the latest I could ever remember of sleeping. It must have been close to eight o'clock. I could hear chickens cackling, calves bawling, and pigs squealing for something to eat.

Mom told William to get some fresh eggs from the hen house for breakfast. I thought I was getting royal honors given to me, all this kind talk and letting me lay in bed till I wanted to get up, and not telling me to do anything.

While ordering the others around to do their biddings, Jim and

Dad came on the porch, stomping the snow from their boots and shedding their heavy coats and gloves. Mom told them to wash for breakfast. While we sat there eating, the sun was shining through the big kitchen window and I could feel the warm rays settling on me.

After breakfast, Jim and I fed and watered all the penned and barned animals while Dad milked the cows. The sun kept getting warmer and the snow started melting. Little streams of melted snow started trickling here and there. As they ran they would melt into high drifts of snow, causing them to cave in with a big splash.

At about two o'clock the road off the mountain was nearly cleared of snow. Water was gushing down from the steep hills above it, washing trees, limbs, and mud in its wake, jamming up against some of the narrow places along the road. Really, it wasn't a road, it was a trail through some of the cornfields and woods. It had been rutted out by the big sled runners loaded with stuff to sell in town.

When the run-off slackened, Jim went with me to care for my big blacks. Then we hiked back up the mountain.

Next morning, Mom stirred pretty early, fixing a good breakfast and making some fried egg sandwiches, with biscuits and slices of salt sidemeat on top of the eggs, for Jim's lunch and mine.

Most of the snow had melted and the coal mines were operating today, but most all the roads and around the tipple and store were nothing but chuck holes filled with mud. I got my orders from the mine office directing me what had to be hauled today. It sure was going to be a hard day for my team, having to pull large loads through all this mud.

We made it as easy as we could for the mules by cutting down hauling from double orders to single orders. The day passed fast with so much to haul and with Jim there to make loading and unloading faster and easier.

Jim and I worked like that up till Christmas. I was paying him according to what I made with the team, and that was more than he had made working for the company.

It was now the day before Christmas. The mines were closing for an extra three days for the holidays. I gave Dad $100 for helping me on the wagon before Jim started. I also gave Jim some extra money to spend on his wife.

Jim just kept talking about what a good, loving woman he had. Sometimes he would go into details about it, explaining everything. We were getting along good working together. I was a little taller than him but not hardly as heavy. He told me that Dad had often told him how he hated himself for the way he had always treated me and how he wished I'd come back home. He had thought I wouldn't stay away over a day or two. Sometimes he'd say that I'd never come back to the mountain.

Christmas was a happy day. Mom and Dad had spent all the money I gave them on nice things for the children and a few things for the house. Jim went overboard buying things for Lilian and wound up owing over a hundred dollars for things that she didn't like or need.

Artie and Amos stayed with us Christmas night, and the whole family stayed up singing Christmas songs, except me. My voice sounded like a bullfrog croaking. I didn't even try to sing. Jim and Lilian sure could. They'd get a song started and then everybody would pitch in. They sang and talked and laughed till after midnight, then they started opening gifts.

Everyone was pleased with what they got. I had gotten everyone a nice but not expensive gift, just something they could use or wear. I got Artie and Amos two nice linoleums for their kitchen and sitting room. They didn't know about what I'd gotten them until they went back home. The store where I got them was to leave them on their porch Christmas Eve. Artie later gave me a big hug and thanks. It sure did make me happy to see her pleased.

While they were opening their packages and giggling to each other, holding pretty dresses and sweaters up close to them, wondering if they would fit, Mom and Dad were sitting sorta in the back, fumbling with some bright-colored packages with their names printed in gold letters, from me. Dad got a shoebox full of nice socks and some good smelling stuff you put on your face after shaving, and a pocket knife. Mom opened hers and her face beamed when she saw the pretty shoes and dress I got Artie to pick out for her.

Jim and Lilian got some kind of a gift from everyone. I walked over to push a log back in a burning position at the fireplace. As I turned back Artie handed me a large box. She said, "Open it up."

I tore the wrapping off. She had gotten me a complete working outfit of clothes. I hadn't expected to get anything from any of them, so I wasn't surprised when I didn't get anything except from Artie.

We all enjoyed the long Christmas week. My mules had rested up and were raring to be back in the harness. Jim had decided he would get a job at another mine and go to housekeeping there. He thought Lilian and he could do better if they left the mountain.

I got started back to work on Monday after Christmas. I pulled up to the store to get a bite of lunch. A group of night miners were reading a paper with big red headlines. The paper said that big steel mills and factories were closing down all over the country. Banks were going broke, big businessmen were committing suicide. All the farmers in the northwest were burning big silos filled with wheat. Ranchers were slaughtering thousands of cattle. This news came during Christmas, but people living back in the mountains didn't get any news until they came to town or heard someone tell about it that had been to town.

The company I worked for posted on their bulletin board that there would be no more work until further notice and for all employees to report to the pay office the following day. They would be paid in full and would receive an honorable discharge from the owners of this mine.

There were a lot of sad faces around that store. Most of the night workers had drifted to this mine from up north. They didn't have families or kin to fall back on. They just got their pay and grabbed the first way out of these hills.

My foreman halted me before I left the store, telling me not to haul anything until I was notified by him or someone else with the authority to do so. He said I could continue using the barn for my big blacks.

For me, it was bad. I had given away nearly all the money I had. I owed for a large shipment of feed that was to come in the last of next month. The company owed me for the past two weeks' work. All the money I had amounted to the price I paid for my lunch.

Here I was, thinking I had the world by the tail, and I wound up with it having me by the tail.

I drove the team up the hollow to the barn and pulled the wagon under the shed, propped the tongue up, and tended the blacks. I then went slowly up the mountain trying to think this one out.

I had lost my contract to haul goods across the mountain and Mr. Ford wouldn't be handling any liquor. Nobody would have any money to buy with. It was winter, no plowing for the town people till spring. I had enough hay and feed to last nearly to spring, if I fed light. I would have to cancel the order I had placed for feed. There just wasn't any way I could win.

As I walked up the mountain, I kept thinking about them big red headlines and about the people that had nearly starved until the government started sending food into Harlan, and the long coal mine strike. I even commenced to thinking of all the killings and rapings.

A thousand things ran through my mind as I made my way up the mountain.

When I got home, I hated to tell Mom and Dad what had happened, but they wanted to know why I wasn't working. I tried to tell them the best I could about what was going on.

Things had been going smooth since I had come back home. Dad and Mom got to the company store and got whatever they wanted and had it charged to my account. I had told them to do so. They had laid up all sorts of staple foods and new farm seeds for the coming spring.

I talked to Dad about him taking over my mules and wagon, that I didn't think there would be any work for them in town. He said, "I'm going to do a lot of heavy farming this year, and I sure could use them."

Dad and I came off the mountain to get the mules. We rode the two riding horses into town. People were milling around the courthouse in large groups. There were hundreds of coal miners from all over the county. They were trying to find out if anything was being done to get some help to feed their families.

The mining companies where these men worked had closed down without notice, leaving them with less than two days' food in their houses and no money at all. The coal miners had lived good while the mines were operating. Every day the big company stores stocked their shelves with all kinds of expensive groceries and meats. The dry goods side of the store was filled with pretty clothes and expensive shoes. The company would stock their store with all these good things to attract the miners to spend their money as they made it. Keeping them without funds and eager to continue to work would keep them from idleness and strikes.

In about a week Amos and Artie moved in with us. They had used up all the food and money they had. Jim and Lilian were still there. Narciss and Sophia, being crowded with all of the rest of the family taking up space in their rooms, decided to go to Ohio and work in restaurants.

When reports reached Washington about all the children and elderly people dying from starvation, they started up programs for the ones able to work and gave free food and clothing for the sick and elderly.

Now, Dad never did have a lot of fancy living things. Him being a mountain man, he managed for Mom and all the rest of the family to do producing work around the farm. Every spring he would have what he called a new ground. All the trees and undergrowth would be piled and burnt. This was where he raised beans and all other vegetables for canning and drying. If a bad season came, Mom would have enough food stored for another year, with plenty to spare. He always made do with what he had to do with.

Jim, Amos, and I spent the rest of the winter clearing a large new ground, using the big blacks to drag logs from it. Dad and Amos would burn brush piles on top of stumps. This left a dark, rich soil; you could grow anything on it. Some folk would say it was so rich you could raise doorknobs on it.

We worked hard getting the ground cleared all the rest of the winter. Spring came and we started plowing the big cornfields for planting. We worked the big blacks single, one to a plow. They acted like they were born for that kind of work.

I helped get the planting done and a lot of cleaning up around the barns. I hauled the manure in a high runner sled and scattered it among tater hills that had just started peeping from the ground. The barn roof had sagged in from the weight of the winter's snow and was leaking in several places. A lot of boards had to be rived to repair it. A new shed was to be built over the well.

Every morning Dad would tell me what I was to do this day. I would try to do every bidding he told me, and wondered why he didn't put Jim or Amos to helping me. Every day when I came to lunch Jim and Lilian would be setting out under a big apple tree or stuck off somewhere by themselves, hugging and kissing.

Amos would be fumbling around in the house, helping Artie and Mom change furniture, clean walls, and sand the floors of the big sitting room. Dad was running around the wooded hill behind the house, hunting for nests of eggs the hens would hide in hollow logs and thickets.

It was coming to where I kept thinking I'd better find out why I was to do all this work and all the rest were to sit around on their asses. After supper, I asked Dad about it. Dad looked at me across the table and said, "If you don't like the way I'm running things my way, the road you came back on, you can leave on."

It's hard for me to put into this writing how I felt when he told me that. I sat there, all the family glaring at Dad and then at me, not saying a word.

I got up from the table, trembling and feeling weak. I had never disobeyed anything Dad ever told me. I was always trying to do things better each time he told me than I had done them before, trying to get some sort of kindness or a good word from him. I had never loved him or Mom, although I didn't hate them. There just wasn't any room in me for love.

My brothers and sisters often showed kindness and some care for me. But the most of the time I felt like a dog's fifth leg when I was around the whole family, except Artie.

I went towards the door and grabbed an old sweater of mine I had hung on the back of the door. I didn't say anything as I went out. This was the second time I had been told to leave the mountain, only now I was nearly grown and had become very strong. I would be fifteen years old this month, July 10. It was now the second day of July.

It was getting late as I left the house. The sun was just going over the western top of the big mountain. I went stumbling down by the barn. I wanted to look in on the big black mules.

I opened their door and walked around them, rubbing their noses and patting them on the neck, talking to them like they understood every word I said. These mules and Artie were the only things I had ever loved. I thought of saying good-bye to them, but somehow I couldn't make it come out right. I just patted each one on the hip as I went out the door.

When I got to the company barn at the foot of the mountain, it was dark. No moon was shining; it was pitch black in the barn. I found the ladder to the loft and climbed it. There was a lot of hay left up there so I crawled under a thick bunch and slept.

NINE

I WOKE UP the next morning and started thinking what to do. There wasn't any work anywhere in Harlan County that you could make a dime at. I walked on into town. It was early when I got there but there must have been thousands of people lined up and down the streets, with big canvas sacks folded under their arms, shivering under the coolness of the early morning air. They were waiting for the big doors to open at the food commodity warehouse. They would receive food to rush back to many homes throughout the county where there were hungry and sick children and parents.

I made my way to the little restaurant and got me some breakfast. The cook at the oil-burning grill was JoJo. That sure shook me up a mite. He told me that him being the youngest employee on the county road gang made him the first one to be laid off. I told him I was hungry and wanted to eat anything he could fix.

He sure fooled me. In about four or five minutes he brought a plate loaded with a big pile of real golden fried taters, two eggs that looked like two big eyes staring at me, four or five strips of good, lean, fresh bacon, and a big blue granite cup of steaming coffee. I told JoJo he'd make some woman a good wife, the way he could cook.

I had kept a little money, not letting anyone know I had it. They would have asked for it if they'd known I had a dime. I had given them everything I had made working for the coal company. I pulled out my Bull Durham tobacco sack and counted what I had. It amounted to nearly $15. I paid for my breakfast out of the silver and bought me a sack of North State smoking tobacco. It all came to thirty cents.

I hadn't smoked around Mom or Dad, but now I wished I had. Jim had started smoking in front of them when he was twelve, but he was the apple of Dad's eye.

I left the restaurant. I wandered off up the street to see what was causing such a crowd in a big field. It looked like there must have been over three thousand people gathered.

A big fat man was standing on a flat-bedded wagon waving his arms for the people to quiet down. He wanted their attention for a few minutes. He rattled on for nearly an hour, telling what great things he had done and how he planned to do a lot of great things for Harlan County in the future if he could get their support in the coming election. He promised the people everything but the moon. For a minute there, I thought he was going to offer them that, too.

Most of this mass of people had brought their canvas sacks with them to receive their government-issued food. Some of the coal companies had started reopening their mines.

Mr. Ford and the ex-sheriff were standing at the rear of the crowd, listening to the fat man make his promises. They shook their heads to each other, like they didn't believe a word he was saying.

Mr. Ford saw me and came up to where I was standing. He asked about the big blacks. I told him everything, all about them telling me to leave the mountain and me giving Dad the team. Mr. Ford said, "That's a damned shame." The former sheriff said the same thing, and then some words I better not write. I sure felt good having such men as these two for friends.

Mr. Ford asked me to go home with him. He said that he would like for me to make it my home till I decided what I wanted to do. I thanked him and said it was nice of him asking me. We said goodbye and then parted.

As I walked through town I started thinking what in the hell was happening to me. Here I was, a grown man nearly, and didn't have a damn thing but the clothes on my back and a little over $14 in my pocket. I was trying to make up my mind of what to do. I was sure having a hard time doing so.

Before I knew it, I was standing on Mrs. Walters' front porch. Then I wondered if I should go on in. I knew that I would be welcomed to stay there for a while. So I knocked at the door and she came to let me in.

Mrs. Walters was a kindly woman, always listening to someone else's troubles and never saying anything about hers. She led me to the kitchen and offered me a chair, then a big glass of cold milk with a large piece of dried apple stack cake.

I sat there wiping my mouth and hands on the sleeves of my

sweater. She sat down across from me, looking me right in the eyes, and said, "It's happened again, hasn't it?"

I nodded my head. Mrs. Walters jumped up and ran her fingers through her hair and seemed to shout to someone else. "What in the world is your people made from?" She said, "If I ever hear of you going back home, I will have JoJo to hold you while I bust your bottom." She added, "You can stay here as long as you want to."

I loafed around town the next day real early, watching the town open up for the Fourth of July. Storemen and the politicians were putting up flags and placing big flat-bedded wagons, all decorated in red, white, and blue with shiny paper, to stand on and make promises and tell lies to all the people who would come to hear them.

People started coming into town on horseback and mules, some walking from way back in the mountains. The L. & N. Railroad put a long line of passenger coaches up the three main forks of the Cumberland River, all decorated up, to bring miners and their families to hear the election speeches and watch some fireworks late in the evening. A lot of stores were giving away free balloons and some were giving small children cones of ice cream.

The politicians were handing out little four-inch U.S. flags, with a big handshake and a pat on the back. One of them would say that he was the only candidate that could do anything for our country. He would then give the person he was talking to a handful of little cards with his picture on it, stating what he intended to do when he got elected to office. Then, with a final handshake, with maybe a $5 or $10 bill in his palm, he would tell the person to talk to his friends and give them one of his cards. He would then go through the crowd looking for another victim.

The idle miners' wives came to town dressed in pretty, bright clothes they had bought from the company stores back when the mines were working.

Nearly every family had brought a basket of food, for it was to be an all-day celebration. I ate at the little restaurant at dinner time. The eating area was small and it stayed jam packed all day, mostly with children eating hamburgers and drinking strawberry pop. All the children that could get near a candidate were given a quarter and then they would dash for the little restaurant for the five-cent hamburgers and nickel pop. JoJo's boss had stocked his whole kitchen with big boxes of buns and he must have stocked a hundred cases of pop.

After hearing all the speeches and watching the largest gathering of people that ever came to the town of Harlan parade through the streets to listen to promises of a bright tomorrow, I worked my way through the crowd of people back to Mrs. Walters'.

It was getting dark when I got there. All the family were sitting lined up on the big porch, waiting to watch the fireworks display. I sat on the stoop and told them of all the speeches I'd heard and about what a big crowd of people had come to town.

For the next few days I loafed around town trying to find some kind of work. But I wasn't the only one hunting a job. The married men were getting the government aid and the town streets stayed filled with groups of boys near my age, most of them from nearby coal camps, who had nothing to do but loaf.

I got with a bunch from the coal camp where I had worked and started roaming up and down the streets. Most of them didn't have a cent in their pockets and hadn't had for a good while. Some of them would make crazy suggestions of ways to make some money. Others suggested leaving Harlan and going to some city to get a good job, save their money, and come back rich. We loafed around day after day. One morning we all met at the L. & N. Railroad water tank.

We walked up and down the side of the railroad, searching for an empty boxcar. We found one with the sliding door about half open and climbed in it. We shut the door real quick and started feeling for a place to sit down.

It was black dark when we closed the door. When we got settled, no one made a sound. We were afraid the railroad dick (that's what everybody called a railroad detective) would come along and throw us off or maybe take us to jail. We sat there real quiet while the engine was taking on water. Finally we felt the car lurch and heard the wheels screak and squeal from the tight-gauged rails on the curves as we went rolling down the line to some great city to get a job and come back rich.

There were seven of us on this venture and most of us had never been out of Harlan County. Arly, one of our group, had hoboed to Cincinnati twice. We huddled around Arly, listening to him tell of his adventures in the city.

Arly said, "My throat got sunburned from looking up so much at the tall buildings. Some streets was so wide you could play a ball game in it. The big rich-looking people rode in big black shiny cars, with a black man driving, wearing a policeman's clothes and it looked like a policeman's cap."

Ott, another of our group, said, "I bet it was a body guard or a gun thug from Harlan doing the driving."

Arly kept talking about the wonders of the city till all of us were wishing we were there now. The train kept moving along, going slowly up steep grades, and when it started down the other side it really picked up speed. The car we were riding in would sway from side to side till I thought it would turn over. Faster and faster it would travel. Some of us would sit in the open door and try to count fenceposts as we passed them. This was the fastest I had ever seen anything move. Every now and then I would wonder if going through all this just to get rich was worth all the thoughts of wrecks, of being derailed, or of the railroad detectives beating us up or taking us to jail.

The train came to a big railroad yard and started slowing down. We closed the door and went to the rear of the car and covered ourselves with some torn-up crates and pasteboard boxes. About the time we got hid, the train stopped moving.

Arly said, "Lay real still till the train starts moving."

We lay there with all this rubbish piled on us, it seemed like for an hour. Arly kept whispering, telling us what to do if we were discovered. If someone else made a whispering suggestion, Arly would say, "Damn it, hush and listen to me. I've been through this before."

About that time, we could hear men talking. They were dicks and were searching the train for hoboes. The door to our car started sliding open and a man poked his head in and shined a bright flashlight to each end of the car. I laid there afraid to breathe, with one eye peering at the light. I wasn't trembling, but I sure felt like I was. The man with the light said, "Ain't nothing in thisun but a damn pile of trash." I sure felt some ease come over me!

The dicks went on down the long line of cars, searching and muttering to each other. The engineer released the brakes and the sound of the escaping air caused every one of us to jump up out of our hiding place, scared stiff.

I peeped my head out the door. I could see the detectives going on down beside the train. We slid the door shut and the train started jerking and backing a little, then jerking again to get all the air brakes released. After a few jerks, the train started rolling off.

It was dark by now. As we went rolling out of the Corbin yards, we opened the door. Some of the boys sat in the door opening, letting their feet hang out, singing old hobo songs and mountain songs.

As the train kept rolling on, we went through town after town, the train never letting up on its speed, the engineer blasting out with the whistle and the bell ringing. The train moved through these towns and counties, sounding its approach and leavings.

The next morning, as the train pulled into Decoursey Yards at Covington, we jumped from the car and ran to a big drain culvert. Crawling through the culvert, we were now outside the railroad property. A stream ran alongside of the fence and a lot of big shady trees lined the banks. We couldn't be seen by anyone unless they were hunting for us. We stripped our clothes off and rinsed them out clean, then jumped in. With mud for soap, we got fairly clean.

While we laid around in the grass, naked as jaybirds, waiting for our clothes to dry enough to put back on, I mentioned that today I was fifteen years old. Instead of my friends wishing me a happy birthday, they grabbed me and then threw me in the stream, laughing all the time they were doing it.

It was about six or seven miles from where we were to Cincinnati. We put our clothes on, hardly dry, and got on a road leading to Ohio.

As we came to the edge of a little village, Arly said we had better split up and go through in pairs, at different times, but to stay on the road number 127. He said, "I'll start alone and wait up at the big bridge where it crosses the Ohio River." He would then direct us to a transit home in Cincinnati.

Arly started, then about ten minutes later me and Ott started. The others followed the same way. As Ott and I got nearly through the village, my belly started to cramp from hunger. I told Ott how I felt and he said, "Arly told me we would be fed at the transit house."

I looked ahead and saw a big store sign. I told Ott I had some money and was going to get something to eat. I showed him my sack. I had $4.80.

I got a loaf of bread, not sliced, a pound of bologna, and two bottles of Nehi pop. I picked up a big onion and asked the man how much I owed. He added it up and said it was thirty-seven cents if I took the bottles, but if we drank them there it would be thirty-five cents.

Ott and I went down the road, him carrying the poke and pop and me slapping thick pieces of bologna on big hunks of bread. We didn't even stop while we ate. We were anxious to see Cincinnati. We had a little meat and bread left when we came to where Arly was sitting on the bridge railing. I offered him the bread and meat.

The rest of our group finally came and Arly gave close instructions so we wouldn't attract attention. He warned us to just glance at the things we had never seen and to be sure to watch for light signals when crossing a street. If we acted strange to the policemen they would take us in and question us.

We made it to the transit house without too much notice, but it was hard not to look up at the tall buildings and gaze at the brightly dressed policemen riding pretty, fancy-stepping horses. Even the horses' hooves looked like they had been polished.

The people walked so fast as they passed you, you didn't have time to say howdy to them. Back home in our town, if you didn't say howdy or something else as you passed on the streets, they'd think you were insulting them or trying to ignore them. But this being a strange place, and the people all strangers to us, we thought we'd act just like them.

By following Arly's directions we came to the street the transit house was on. It was a beautiful building. There were wide steps going up to a long flat, wide place and another bunch of steps going on up to a big wide porch. Along the edge of the porch about eight or ten big white posts supported a huge covering. At the back of the porch, on each side of the large doors, pictures of pretty women, birds, and other things were made right into the concrete wall. The glass in the windows had every color of the rainbow in them. I thought the boxcar ride was well worth it, just to see this one building.

We all grouped together and lined up at a big desk. A motherly looking lady with bluish-looking hair and a big smile on her face sat behind it and said, "Welcome to our station."

She handed each of us a card to fill out that would show where we were from, where we were going, how long we intended to remain there, and a lot of other questions we didn't know how to answer.

A big colored man came up to the desk and said for us to follow him. He led us through a big hallway and lounge rooms filled with relaxed looking people sitting in large couches and chairs and long-backed sofas. These were people stopped here to get a free meal and a night's lodging, just like we were doing.

The man led us to a large shower room, showed us to the towel rack, and said for us to get clean, then to wash our clothes. After that he would assign each of us to a bunk to wait for our clothes to dry.

We got our clothes from the drying room. They smelled with some kind of disinfectant, like sulphur or something real strong, to keep down the spreading of odors and diseases people brought in.

We dressed in our clean clothes and then an alarm sounded. Everyone started lining up to go from the lounge room down a long hallway to a big open kitchen to be fed. The station would give each person two meals a day for five days, then no more for ten days. When your five days were up, you turned your tag in to the office. After the ten days, you could register for another five days of free food and a place to sleep.

The food they gave us for supper was good. The men doing the serving of the tray would dish on according to our size and how hungry we looked. We got a big square of cornbread, a large tin cup of milk or coffee, boiled cabbage, a good serving of mashed taters, and some applesauce with a little piece of cake laying on top of it. A good sized piece of meat lay beside the taters. We sure enjoyed this meal.

After the supper was over we went in pairs up and down the streets looking at all the beautiful things we had never seen before— big electric clocks built right into the front of buildings, store windows with real lifelike dummies of men and women dressed in the prettiest clothes I had ever seen.

I told Ott this was too big of a place for me. The only thing I knew how to do was drive a team or work on a farm, and I was going to head back to Harlan in the morning.

The city was lightening up for the night people. Fast-blinking lights started making arrows and pointers, directing people to their entrances.

The next morning, after having a good breakfast, our group met in the lounge room and decided to go back to Harlan. As we passed the lady at the desk, we handed her our tags and thanked her for the kindness she had shown us. I told her we were giving up the city life. She smiled as we turned to leave.

We had no trouble at all getting from Ohio to the Corbin yards. We looked in a car that had been loaded with canned foods and candy. We loaded ourselves with dented cans and bursted boxes of candy and walked across several tracks to where a small switch engine was making up a train of boxcars to be pulled through Harlan. All the others decided they'd go to Louisville, but not me. I thought I'd had enough of hoboing to last me a lifetime.

They left me there and headed for the other end of the yard. Pretty soon the train got made up and a big black mally came steaming, its bell ringing. The engineer's head and shoulders were sticking through the window. He had a striped long-bill cap setting square on his head and a big red bandana tied around his neck, blasting his whistle in short bursts to clear the tracks as the mally made its way to the front of the made-up train.

An oiler showed me the only empty car in the train. It was a low-sided car, billed to go to Virginia, right through Harlan. I climbed into the gon and got settled down, waiting to feel the movement of the train. It started off smoothly, picking up speed slowly. By the time it got out of the yard the wheels were making a clicking sound as they passed over the rail joints. I lay down, placing my sweater wrapped up for a pillow, and soon fell asleep.

I must have slept for over an hour. A long, lonesome wailing sound came from the whistle of the big mally as it went around the curves and up the grades, and it brought me awake.

I lay there feeling the sway of the car and listening to the clickety clack as the wheels passed over each rail joint. I stared at the stars, just letting my mind drift backwards, and then started thinking what I was going to do with myself in the future. My eyes were getting heavy and I started dozing. I tried to stay awake to be able to continue thinking, but I drifted off to sleep. When I awoke the train was slowing down. It was nearly daylight. The engineer sounded his whistle and started his bell to ring, giving warning of his approach into the yard. I peeped over the side of the gon and tried to find some kind of sign to let me know how much further it was to Harlan. The train was barely moving and the bell continued ringing.

The train passed a little depot. On the front were the words "Hagans, Virginia." I thought, "What in the world am I doing here? I wanted to get off in Harlan!" Here I was, about thirty-five miles past Harlan and no roads going back over the mountains for another twenty miles. The only way back for me was through three long tunnels and I was so hungry I could eat the south end of a north-bound skunk.

I looked out over the top of the car and saw a man hooking a big horse to a plow. I climbed out and crossed the tracks to where he was and asked him, "Where might a fellow get something to eat?"

He motioned for me to come over. I climbed the fence and came up to him. He was a big man with large, rough-looking hands. His mustache hung down to his chin and his eyebrows met; they were jet black. Along his neck were deep wrinkles. His hair, just a little bit gray, covered part of his ears. This was a true mountain man, living under the fear of God's mighty hand and knowing of the great love He has for men on earth. I stood there for a moment, just staring at him, hoping to someday become as strong and fearless looking as this man.

He asked if what he had heard the railroad men say about Harlan was true. He mentioned a few things about the killings, rapes, and people starving. I told him it was all the truth. He said, "You're sure welcome to my house." He unhooked the big horse and turned it back in the barn and said, "Let's go up to the house."

It was a big, sprawling log house with a very low ceiling. It had a wide porch going all the way around. The lady of the house had pots of flowers and climbing red roses from each end of the front porch. Two big June apple trees were in the front yard, hanging full of pretty red and green striped apples. Along the fence were rows of bee hives.

I followed him in, walking careful so as not to step on a hound pup, one of a litter of ten. They were just beginning to crawl about, just waddling around. He showed me to the wash stand and asked if I wanted to wash up a mite. I washed my face and hands and then poured a lot of water over my head to wash the cinders from my hair. While riding the train, the cinders and black smoke would settle all behind the engine as it puffed it high in the air.

I stood before a big cracked mirror and combed my red hair. As I stood there I looked at myself. I didn't see a scrawny kid, I looked more like a man. Ever since they ran me off the mountain the first time, I felt I'd become a man.

The big man came through the door and asked if I was ready to sit. I followed him back through the door. The lady, his wife, was setting me a plate. She brought me two hotcakes, one covered with creamy gravy, and two big fried eggs laying beside it. A large glass of milk was handed to me. I tried to eat with a little manners, but my hunger outdid them.

While I was eating, the man told me his name was Roy Creech. He had been born and raised right here on this farm. He had been the only child. He had married and remained there to live out his life. He said, "The only news I get is mostly from the railroad men and that is just once in a while, since the train only stops every now and then."

I pulled my tobacco sack out and poured my bankroll out on the table. I had two one-dollar bills, three quarters, and four pennies. I asked the lady if I could pay her for my food. As I laid a dollar over near her, Mr. Creech said, "Absolutely not! I welcomed you to my table, not for pay. You said you were hungry and I had plenty to feed you and I'm proud to have you sit at my table."

I thanked them kindly and rose to leave. He came to the door with me and started telling me of shortcuts and different trails over the three big mountains back to Harlan. He said, "A lot of the climbing will be mighty rough. I don't think you could make it across them in less than two days." He then asked me if I would like to stay around helping him do the work here. He said, "I can't pay you no money, but you sure wouldn't ever be hungry."

We had walked out to the porch as we talked and he started pointing to different fields, some with corn about knee-high that needed plowing, and two big bottoms of oat hay that had to be mowed, dried, and stacked. A lot of the fenceposts had to be replaced and he needed to start bringing in firewood for next winter.

Now don't get me wrong. He fed me a breakfast and I was grateful to him for it and offered to pay for it. But I couldn't see why I should stay there all summer and work for just my keep. I was now over fifteen years old and I needed to do a lot of planning. If I meant to get any older, I better start now.

I told Mr. Creech I had been on my own for the past three years and had come to a hard place for me to get straightened out. But I aimed to look up some good friends I had in Harlan and try to get started back to driving a team for one of them. Mr. Creech said, "I sure wish you luck, but you are welcome to stay here if you want to."

He said it might be a little dangerous but he thought I could make it faster and easier if I walked back to Harlan through the three tunnels. He didn't think another train would be coming through for several more days.

I thanked him again and shook hands to bind friendship, for I sure wanted to remember him as a friend. Mrs. Creech handed me a wrapped package. She said, "I'd like for you to take this." It was all she could put together in such a short time and I was welcome to have it. I didn't do it, but I wanted to give her a hug and a kiss. I just turned red. I shook her hand and thanked her and then started towards the railroad.

After I climbed the fence, Mr. Creech and his wife were in the yard waving at me. I started off down the tracks headed for the tunnels. It was a good ten miles to the first one, the rails making long curve after curve.

The sun was shining hot and the reflections from the white limestone ballast rock and the rails were blinding. The sweat kept running down my face and started burning my eyes. I thought I'd better take it a little easier. I didn't have anything to rush back to. I looked ahead and saw the entrance of the first tunnel.

I finally made it to the big gaping hole and could feel cool air coming from it. I stood in the center of the track, looking into the dark hole. I could see a small light about the size of a pinhead. It was the light of day through the tunnel. A stream of cold water was flowing from the tunnel.

I sat down near the entrance, letting the cool air come sweeping around me. After cooling and resting my feet and legs for a few minutes, I unwrapped the package Mrs. Creech had given me. My belly was telling me it was hungry. It kept growling like a bulldog.

After satisfying my stomach I knelt down on my knees and took a long cool drink. I rewrapped my food cloth and stood looking the tunnel in the eye. The light spot hadn't gotten any larger. I was standing there, deciding how to handle this. It was a scary looking problem. I'd never been inside a cave or underground before.

I slipped my sweater on and fastened my wrapped food inside it. There was a walkway beside the track going in the tunnel, but I didn't know how far in it would last. I thought a long stick should come in handy to guide me on the rails as I walked through. I found one laying over by a creek, about five foot long with a knob on the end.

I then entered that hole. It was around twenty foot high and looked like ten to twelve foot wide, with little potholes along the sides.

I kept in the walkway, using my stick for a guide. Every now and then I'd stumble on a block of coal or a big boulder that had fallen from the roof. I'd cuss at it a little and keep on, feeling my way with the stick.

I'd gone about five hundred yards, listening for shale or rocks falling from the roof, when all of a sudden a big flapping noise went by me. Then it seemed like there were hundreds of them flapping past me, some brushing against me as they passed. That shook me up so that my hair was standing up like bristles. I was so scared I nearly shit in my overalls. It was so sudden I didn't have time to realize it was bats I had disturbed.

I kept feeling my way, and the light at the other end was getting bigger and bigger. Soon I was through the first tunnel. I looked back through it and silently thanked the Lord for letting me make it. I sat down on the end of a tie and leaned back on a rail, and stretched my legs out to stop them from quivering. I looked into the sky to judge the time of day.

I couldn't see the sun, the mountains being so tall and steep and the valley so narrow the sun didn't hang overhead for more than thirty or forty minutes.

The track made a sharp curve after leaving the tunnel. I followed it for about four or five miles, looking for a safe place to sleep and to eat some more of my food. I spotted a large overhang just ahead and made for it. I climbed the steep bank and found what I'd been looking for. I stomped the weeds down and smoothed them out level as I could. I then opened my food wrapper and ate a goodly half of what I had. There were two hoe-johnnies slapped together with blackberry jam. They sure did taste good.

It was now getting dark. I laid down on the soft weeds and soon fell asleep. I didn't sleep long before I started chilling and shaking. I'd roll the warm side up till it got cold, then I'd roll over and warm the other side. I kept this up all night. When morning came I was more tired than when I laid down. I sat up, looked all about me, rubbing my eyes to get the sleep from them. Then I started scooting and sliding down the bank.

It was now light enough for me to get started. I picked up my stick and started walking. I began to count the ties. After counting several hundred, I began walking on top of a rail and counting ties at the same time.

I soon came to the next tunnel. It looked just like the one I had come through. I sat down and finished my hoe-johnny and jam, then started looking for an easy way to get down to the creek. That dry hoe-johnny had my mouth feeling like I'd been chewing cotton. I needed a drink of that cool-looking water.

When I finally got to the creek, I wet my face with icy cold water, trying to ease the burning in my eyes, then I started handing water to my mouth. I must have drunk eight or ten big handfuls of water, letting some of it spill down the bib of my overalls.

I made my way back up, over boulders that had been blasted from the face of the tunnel, and got started through. I was hoping I wouldn't get as excited as I did in the other tunnel if something jumped out on me.

I made it through this one a lot better than the first one, although it was longer. The next and last one was just about one mile through it. I could see nearly every step I made.

I was now in Harlan County and about fourteen miles from town. Where I was now, it was downgrade all the way to town. I walked the ties till I came to a spur track that led off up a hollow to the Three Point Coal Company. From here it was three miles to Cawood.

When I got to the village of Cawood it was dark but a few lights were shining in some of the little shops and restaurants. I entered a restaurant and asked if it was too late to get something to eat. The big greasy looking man said, "Not if you got the money to pay for it." I opened my tobacco sack and laid down two quarters. He looked at them and said, "You name it, Bub."

While I was eating my brown beans and fried potatoes with a big hunk of government-relief roast beef and a cup of hot black coffee, Lil Barker came in with a long five-cell flashlight in his hand. He asked the big greasy man if he had flashlight batteries to sell. The man said, "I do." He reached under the counter for them.

Lil unscrewed the light and glanced my way. I was just finishing eating. He came over to me and asked, "What in the hell are you doing up here?"

While he was fitting the batteries I told him how I had slept coming through Harlan Town, and about me walking back through the tunnels from Hagans, Virginia. He and the big greasy man slapped their legs and began laughing.

Lil sat down and had a cup of coffee and told me why he was there so late. Lil drove a Dodge truck for the new wholesale in Harlan. I had done some hauling for them with the big blacks and I knew him quite well. He said I'd be doing him a big favor if I'd ride back to Harlan with him. I said, "I sure would be glad to."

The town of Harlan had the only paved street or road in the county. All the county roads were built and raised with creek rock, sand, and gravel. The only bridge in the county spanned the Clover Fork that flowed through the middle of Harlan. If anyone wanted to cross the river they either used a paddleboat, rode a horse, or swam. The roads to the mining camps up all these hollows and hills had to ford the rivers several times before reaching the last camp in the hollows. When the rivers were in flood stage, after a heavy downpour or a cloudburst, there was no way to travel. You just had to wait till the water went down.

Lil got the flashlight working and he paid for my supper. I picked up my two quarters. We got started out of Cawood, him holding the flashlight with his left arm sticking out the window and trying to shift gears and steer with the other.

This wasn't working very well. He killed his motor several times, then he'd start cursing. He couldn't see the road very well, with the truck bouncing about on the rough road. Finally, after he killed his motor over a dozen times, I asked him if I could lay on the fender and hold the light for him. In this fashion we made it to Harlan. I was laying on my belly, clinging to the cross bar of the headlight with my right hand and with my right leg lying in between the fender and the motor. My legs got so hot I tried to look around to see if they were smoking.

Lil parked the truck under the loading dock, got his possible bag, and said, "I'll have a hell of a time trying to explain to my wife for being so damn late. I'd like you to come spend the night at my house and back up my excuses." I accepted his offer, it being so late I didn't want to wake up the Walterses.

When we got to his home, his wife met us at the door. She asked, "What in the world happened? I've been worried sick about you. You should have sent me word of what's happened."

Lil started patting her shoulder and telling her, "Everything's all right. I just had trouble with my headlights, ain't that right, Red?"

I said, "It's the truth, just look at my overall leg." It had oil from my thigh to my shoe, black with it. That must have convinced her. She asked me to come on in the house.

She had Lil's supper setting in the warming closet of the big cookstove. He washed his hands and then motioned with his head for me to do the same. We sat down and she set his supper on the table. I had eaten at Cawood, but riding on my belly on that rough bumpy road had beat it out of me. I accepted a plate and dug in. She was an excellent cook and the food was good.

Mrs. Barker looked at the oil on my leg. She handed me a large pan of warm water and told me to follow her. We went to a little off room with a small bed and a chair and a vanity dresser with a mirror big as a door.

She laid some of Lil's clothes on the bed and said, "Throw your oily clothes out to me and you be sure you wash all the oil off you.

It might cause your leg to get sore. Then put the clean clothes on."
I sure hadn't expected to get this kind of treatment.

After taking a pan bath, I got into Lil's clothes and went in to sit with them. They wanted to know about my hobo trip. Lil already knew about me and my family. We sat there for over two hours, me telling of the things I had seen and how the city folks stared at us like we were animals. I just guess they did think it, the way we were going through the streets, staring and gawking at everything we saw.

I went to bed in the room where I had bathed. The next day being Sunday, Lil said, "Sleep till you're ready to get up." I fell asleep at once.

TEN

AT THE CRACK of dawn I was wide awake. The room started getting lighter as the sun kept rising. It looked like this was going to be a beautiful day. I laid there till I heard voices. I got out of bed and went to the kitchen.

Mrs. Barker was folding my clothes. They had dried hanging behind the big stove. I took them back to the room where I had slept. She had ironed my shirt and my overalls. They had shined from her pressing the iron on them. I wiped my shoes clean. When I came back in, Lil said, "Boy, you sure look different this morning."

Mrs. Barker had breakfast almost ready. I hurried and washed my face, wet my hair and combed it. I felt real clean.

We ate a good breakfast and sipped an extra cup of coffee. They wanted me to stay the day with them, but I wanted to see Dave Good or Mr. Ford. I got up from the table and thanked them and left.

I went to the livery stable and asked Uncle John about getting a horse. I told him I wanted to ride out to Mr. Ford's. He said, "Dave Good brought three of Ford's Morgans in yesterday to have them all reshod by the blacksmith and their hooves trimmed good. It would save Mr. Good a trip if you'd take them for him."

I climbed up on a big bay, Uncle John handed me the lead line, and I started off. I hadn't seen Mr. Ford for a while.

Mr. Ford and his wife were sitting under a big shade tree when I rode up. They didn't see me until one of the horses snorted. He looked up with a surprised look on his face and said, "Damn if it ain't Red. Get down, get down, come on over here."

He looked me up and down and said, "Boy, you sure have grown up a lot." He started squeezing my shoulders and arms and said, "You're solid as a rock. Let's put the horses in the lot, then I want to hear all about you."

I guess if a fellow ever had a friend, I had one. We sat there over an hour, me telling everything that had happened to me since I last saw him.

He said he had sold all his stock but seven head. I asked about the lame one, Old Bob. He said, "The split hoof never grew back good. I traded him for a good five-gaited six-year-old mare, purtiest thing you ever seen and gentle as a pup."

Mrs. Ford had gone in the house and left us sitting there talking. Mr. Ford didn't mention Dad or the big blacks and I didn't either. He asked me if I had any plans. I shook my head no. He went on, telling me he had a contract to haul a lot of building materials over the mountain and he had a team for me if I was interested in it.

I can't explain how I felt. Goose pimples ran up and down my back. My face tingled. I just felt good all over when he told me this. I told him that this must be my lucky day, and I'd sure be pleased to drive for him. That's about what I said. I was so glad to get this job that I don't remember.

Mrs. Ford came out and said, "Dinner will be ready shortly, so wash up." I knew I was to get a good meal at her table, and I sure did that day.

Mr. Ford asked me if I was going to stay at Mrs. Walters'. If I wasn't he'd like me to stay there with them when I wasn't hauling. I could work around the farm.

Every time he mentioned something, it fit right in with me. I said, "I'd like to get some things from Mrs. Walters' and a few things in town tomorrow. I'd be ready to start Tuesday."

"That's fine," he said. "We'll get you a wagon ready and you can start a trip Thursday, if we don't have any hitches."

I thought I'd better get started back to town so I could make plans. I got up and thanked them both and started for the door.

Mr. Ford said, "Hold on there a minute, you. Are you aimin' to walk to town?"

I said, "Yes, sir."

He said, "Like hell you will. You get that riding horse and leave her at the livery and bring yourself back tomorrow."

I got the mare and put one of them fancy saddles on her. Some people called them English saddles. It didn't even have a horn on it, just a little chunk of leather with fancy looking stitches and a tiny belly girth, not even a boot at the stirrup. I didn't say anything, but I thought Mr. Ford was getting sorta citified, riding around in a town saddle. He was always the rugged type to me.

When I got back to town, I got a dry-goods store to let me owe for twenty-five dollars' worth of clothes and two pair of boots. I had left everything I had on the mountain except what I had on and my old sweater. I'd worn my boots plump through at the sole, and the toe on the left one just covered my toes. It had worn loose from the sole and would flop every step I'd take. It took a lot of explaining to the store man to credit me, but I had hauled a lot of big boxes of new clothes across the mountain for him and he knew me pretty well.

Mr. Ford was at the harness shed working on an old set of harness when I got back from town the next morning. He had two big leather collars he was aiming to patch. Half the padding had come out of them from big holes worn through the leather by the hame lugs. He was cutting out broken and worn strips of leather and replacing them with other strips worn just about as bad.

As I hopped down from the mare, Mr. Ford said, "I thought I'd fix your team up with a good set of harnesses. Them trips over the mountains sure do tear and wear on a harness."

I looked at what he had been working on and shook my head. I said, "Mr. Ford, this set of harness wouldn't last to pull an empty wagon over the mountain." I lifted one of the collars and the walls fell together. The padding had nearly all sifted through the worn holes.

Mr. Ford laid his bradding hammer down and scratched his head and then scratched his butt. (He was always scratching his butt.) He said, "That's the only set I've got left. I let the good stuff go when I sold the other teams."

I had ridden by Uncle Hamp Huff's shop that morning to get me a bundle of rawhide to make boot laces, and I had looked at two long walls lined with shiny new harness, tassels hanging on it. I asked Mr. Ford to let me take my team of Morgans to Uncle Hamp's and have them fitted with new harnesses.

He started scratching his butt and thinking. Finally he said, "Go ahead, but I will have to owe Uncle Hamp till the money starts coming in. If Uncle Hamp will put the cost on the books, go ahead and get heavy harness."

I didn't say another word. I unsaddled the mare, turned her out in the barn lot, got two perfectly matched Morgans, and lit out of there for town. I told Uncle Hamp what Mr. Ford had said. Uncle Hamp said, "Ford's word is good enough for anything he wants from my shop."

We walked along the wall, looking at all the heaviest harnesses.

90

I stopped in front of a set. All the hipping and the wide big back band were decorated with bright shiny brass and red, white, and blue tassels. The tugs were an inch thick, the hitching chains extra heavy. This set sure got my eye. I started feeling the leather and flipping a tassel, watching it fall back in place. I asked if he'd fit this set on the Morgans I had out front.

Uncle Hamp looked at me over the tops of his looking glasses and said, "That's the strongest set of harness I ever made and it's the best leather I ever worked with."

We toted the harness out front and got two black twenty-four-inch collars. Then we fitted all the buckles to a good snug fit at every connecting place and put big brass-knobbed hames on the collars. We put black bridles on, with big four-inch blinders. The bridles had little brass brads all over them.

When we got through, we stepped back to get a good look. They sure did look good with all that brass and them tassels shining. I asked Uncle Hamp, "How much does it cost?"

He said, "I'll let Mr. Ford know when he comes to town."

I didn't ride through town, I walked behind, holding the new checkreins and a long, keen leather six-plait hanging from my shoulder, only to use when one of the Morgans failed to obey a command. I sure did walk proud through town. People were hollering at me and asking, "When will the rest of the horse show come through?" I'd just grin and keep going.

It was a good five miles to the Fords' farm, and I walked every foot of the way, feeling ten foot tall. Them big blacks were a pretty matched team, but these Morgans outdid them in looks. I've often wished I'd had a camera back then so I could have had pictures to show you. Please don't think that I'm exaggerating when I try to write of the beauty of these fine animals. These two Morgans were perfectly matched, each having the same markings and each weighed, to everybody's guess, eighteen hundred pounds.

As I walked them out of town I started talking to them, giving commands without using the checkreins, such orders as to yoo, gee, haw, back up, circle one, to hold the other, to start. After going through these commands several times, I'd go up and rub their noses, loosen their bridle reins from the hames, allowing them to move their heads up and down, letting them have a free head. They would sling their heads and chomp on the iron bits. I'd allow this for a few minutes, then go again. This continued until we got to the harness shed.

Mr. Ford saw me walking them up the lane. He came over to the shed and walked around the team, admiring the new harness and all the trimmings. He helped me take the harness from them and hang it in the shed. We then looked at the wagon. He had done a good job putting new canvas over it and had it greased and ready to go.

Mrs. Ford had me a nice room off the kitchen with a door to the outside. I could go and come without disturbing them and it was also an easy way to the warming closet of the stove. She always had food there.

The next morning when Mr. Ford came to the barn, I already had the Morgans harnessed and hitched. I had all my gear stowed in my footlocker and ready to go. It wasn't hardly daylight yet, so we left the team standing and went to the house for breakfast and to get instructions for the trip. Mr. Ford had hired Jesse for my scotcher. JoJo was still slinging hash at the little restaurant.

I drove the Morgans to the lumber yard and loaded my wagon with building materials, such as doors, windows, tar paper, roofing—about anything you needed for building, except foundation stuff. I had a big load, but it wasn't heavy. With Jesse scotching, and having a light load, I made a record-time trip. Mr. Ford was very much pleased about it.

The Morgans were a fine working team. I made about twenty-five trips, hauling mostly building materials over and bringing produce and moonshine back. Some of the trips would take several days to make.

The Fords treated me like family. I never saw Dad or any of the family all summer.

The weather started turning cold. I'd helped put up enough firewood for the winter. Mr. Ford and his help had mowed all the meadows and had plenty of hay for his cattle and horses. They were now filling all the cribs with corn. The brood sows had raised a good crop of porkers.

This was the biggest and most productive farm in Harlan County, and it made me feel awful good to know that the owner and his wife were treating me like I was their son. At that time, and ever since, I've had a deep love for them.

We completed the contract for hauling the material over the mountain and were preparing for a cold winter. We were trying to make caring for everything on the farm handy. We built warm stalls in the cattle barn for the young calves and milk stock to stay in, and a big closed raised ground shed for the feeder herd. Every day we'd make some kind of improvement on the farm. Mr. Ford had paid me good for driving and wanted to pay me for the work I was doing on the farm.

I stayed through the winter with them, taking care of all the feeding and keeping the watering places free after a freeze, trying to keep Mr. Ford from going out in the cold. Twice a week I'd go to town on the mare to check on mail and pick up a few things for Mrs. Ford.

On these trips I always was hoping to see someone of my family. I thought of Artie a lot, specially when I'd been out all day and had the sniffles or a cold. I missed having her come to where I was sleeping and ask if I was warm. I hadn't seen or heard of any of them since I left.

The government was still shipping food and clothing to Harlan County and other surrounding counties. A lot of the coal mines had reopened and the Harlan County Coal Operators' Association was doing the same as before, but they were doing it in a different way. They set up a company union, stating all the great advantages of belonging to it. You got free medical care, all holidays off with pay, a seven-hour work day instead of eight, free coal for heating, and a credit system where you could buy as much as $500 on credit and you would pay a little each day from your earnings.

The H.C.C.O.A. had their hirelings going about the county dressed like big businessmen, flashing big wads of money, buying dinners for large groups of miners that were working on the W.P.A. for food and no money. They were telling them the union they represented was greater and had more influence over the operators than the United Mine Workers of America. They would say, "Now, if you just sign this paper, you'll become eligible to receive all these benefits." Then they'd offer everyone an expensive cigar and a big handshake. The unsuspecting men would sign up with the yellow-dog union.

I would get all the news I could each time I went to town. The Fords were anxious for me to get back and tell all I could learn.

It was now near Christmas and Mr. Ford was about out of whiskey. A lot of the mines had started back to work, more steel mills were operating, and money was being spent more freely. The bootleggers Mr. Ford provided for were demanding more moonshine. The miners wanted good moonshine and were willing to pay a better price.

This got Mr. Ford to do some planning. We sat in the kitchen one night and discussed a way to get a load to have around Christmas time. Mr. Ford would hire a man to take over the chores I was doing.

The cold kept him housed up nearly all the time with a cold and cough and wheezing. Mrs. Ford would fuss at him if he opened the door just to look out. She'd say, "Shut that door. You want to catch your death of cold?" She was always pampering him, making him think he was more sick than he was. Every morning he would have a hot toddy before breakfast. He would pour a large coffee cup half full of moonshine, then add two big spoons of sugar. His wife would then pour boiling water to fill the cup. He would sit there and sip, smacking his lips, enjoying it.

The man he hired was nearly a cripple. He had gotten his foot mashed under a rock fall in a coal mine, causing the foot to form into a mass. It looked more like a box than a foot. His nickname was Club, meaning he had a clubfoot. I showed Club everything that had to be done. He was a good worker and seemed to know a lot about animals.

I left the second day after Club came, to take a load of sugar across the mountain to Mr. Anderson. The Morgans had been taking it easy for a long while and we were ready to work. I got Jesse to go with me. He was eager to get started. He was at the wholesale with rolled-up possibles when I got there.

My wagon was in good shape. I had worked my canvas to give me a covering over the seat. I had never seen one fixed this way before.

We made our trip in three days without any trouble. We brought the usual load back and carried it down into the cellar. We had 600 gallons of the best moonshine that was ever made in the state of Kentucky. That was the message I was to tell Mr. Ford.

The liquor didn't last long. The bootleggers made quick work of it and were wanting more of the same blend. They were selling it for a much better price than before. Mr. Ford got to making bargains with them. The farm-raised foods that were used to hide the liquor— shucky beans, cured hams, dried fruits, and a lot of other stuff— were beginning to crowd every storage place on the farm. For each ten gallons of moonshine they bought, an agreement was made for a few items of the produce that was used to hide it. The bootleggers didn't like the idea at first, but soon some of them were taking double the amount of the farm foods. One bootlegger said, "The miners' women are ordering more of the farm foods than their men are ordering whiskey!" This soon cleared all the storage places.

Mr. Ford put Jesse and me on more trips over the mountain. I guess you could call him the kingpin bootlegger. As for Jesse and me, our title could now be whiskey runners.

The new sheriff was easy for Mr. Ford to buy off. He was getting rich with all the extra money coming in from operators of the coal mines for furnishing them with hand-picked men, trained under him for the art of controlling or pleasing dissatisfied miners in their company union. If for some reason a miner needed a sum of money for an emergency, the trained hireling would always have the ready cash to please him.

Mr. Ford kept Jesse and me hauling all winter and spring. We took enough sugar over the mountains to sweeten the whole county of Harlan. We were loading and unloading at eight or ten different farms. Nearly everybody knew what we were hauling, but they were soon satisfied with a gift or a jug, or maybe a big country ham or middlin of side meat.

The days and nights were getting warmer now. Mr. Ford was stirring about, getting his work hands to shaping up the farm after the cold winter snows and rains had done their damage. He had men plowing and sowing big fields of early hay. Others were plowing and cleaning the hillside cornfields for planting. A crew of builders were putting up a long building to house thousands of laying hens. I guess Mr. Ford was coming to be one of the richest men in Harlan County.

Every now and then Mr. Ford would allow me a day or two off between trips across the mountain. I'd ride the mare and leave her at the livery. Uncle John would care for her while I loafed around town. I would buy a few things here and there. I'd listen to the merchants and other people talk about what was going on all over the country.

I would go see JoJo every time I'd go to town, and fill up on them five-cent hamburgers. Sometimes he'd tell of someone in my family dropping in for a snack. He'd worm some kind of news out of them to pass to me.

Sometimes I'd stay overnight at Mrs. Walters', taking her some kind of a little gift. She was always pleased with whatever I brought her.

With the increase in the number of miners accepting the company union, more demands were being made for moonshine and farm foods. Mr. Ford started another team hauling sugar over and bringing liquor back. He had men coming from out of state with trucks, taking load after load to cities. He had all the law bought off and was selling it wide open.

One day I was in town and met the ex-sheriff. He greeted me and said, "I want to give you some advice." He invited me to sit and talk in the lobby of the big hotel. We looked around for a place to sit away from other people. Pulling a chair out, his back to the others, looking straight at me, he said, "Red, you're about to get in real trouble."

He let that sink in for a minute and then went on to tell me what a good friend he was to Mr. Ford and what kind of friend he wanted to be to me. He said he knew for a fact the federal government was cracking down on the bootlegging in Harlan County. They were to catch me with a load, then move in on Mr. Ford.

He said he knew that I'd had a hell of a life growing up, and hated to see me being used by our friend, Mr. Ford. He told me to break away from him some way, make any kind of excuses to him, and be damned sure I didn't haul any more liquor until this blew over. He said, "I hate like hell to be the one to have to tell Mr. Ford about what I know. I don't want you to let it be known to anyone I told you."

I got my bundle of new clothes and left him sitting there, not facing the other people. If word got out that he had warned me, his chances for the sheriff's office next election would be mighty slim.

It was clouding up and the sky was darkening when I came out on the street. It looked like it was going to be a real downpour.

I started to make my way to the little restaurant to talk to JoJo. He and I had no secrets. A large group of people were crowded inside, drinking coffee and pop, waiting out the storm.

JoJo wiped a small table and held onto a chair, then motioned for me to come and get it. I ordered myself three hamburgers, some taters, and a big glass of buttermilk. It took some waiting to get it, with so many people crowded in there, calling in their orders. I finally got mine. JoJo had fixed a lunch for himself and sat down with me.

I started eating, not saying a word, just glancing from time to time at JoJo. Finally he said, "What in the hell is eatin' on you? You ain't said a damn word since I sat down!"

I just kept on eating. When I'd finished, I started telling him what the former sheriff had told me. I said, "I've decided to quit, and I can't make up my mind what to do or where to go."

JoJo said he had heard about the government going to crack down, but he hadn't heard it the way I had. As far as having a place to stay, I had one. He said, "My Mom said that you were welcomed anytime if you wanted to come back." I sat there for over an hour, listening to all the crowd talking at the same time. My mind was doing some fast planning on how to cope with my problem.

The rain was letting up and the crowd started thinning out. JoJo brought me some coffee for an excuse to speak to me. He didn't want his boss to catch him idling his time with a customer. As he set the cup down, he told me to meet him up the street in front of the hotel when he got off. Then he went back to work.

The rain had stopped but a strong wind was taking its place. As I came through the door it hit me with such force I could hardly move forward. Water was rushing down the street like a river running wild.

I went back in and stood around the book and paper rack, killing time, to wait out the storm. I picked up a paper, the *Knoxville News-Sentinel*. It had big pictures over the front page showing federal agents with captured moonshine stills. The stills appeared to be a lot larger than the ones I had visited across the mountain.

The wind died down and I sauntered off up the street, staring in all the store windows, looking at dummy women and men dressed in pretty summer clothes to attract the eyes of miners and their wives.

When JoJo got off, I met him and we started across town to his home. Mrs. Walters was glad to see me. She wanted to fix me something to eat. I shook my head and told her JoJo had already fed me. We all sat down at her kitchen table and she gave a quick rundown on all the things she thought I might be interested in. Then she said, "Tell me what's been happening to you? You don't look much pert."

I was sitting there, thinking that with friends like this I could trust them with my life. I told her what was bothering me. I told her I had a little money. I thought I'd ride a passenger train to Ohio and visit my two sisters there. I was now grown. I would be sixteen years old in three days. I could do any kind of hard labor, but I didn't want to work in the coal mines.

Mrs. Walters asked me to stay there for a few days before leaving for Ohio. JoJo said he would go with me to Mr. Ford's and help carry my things back. If we left now, we would be back by ten o'clock.

We got started to the livery stable. Uncle John was back along the stalls cleaning up horse droppings. I told him I wanted to rent a horse and buggy to make a trip to Mr. Ford's. I told him I was quitting my job with him, and why I wanted the buggy.

Lee Ball always left his horse there for Uncle John to hire out for him. He made a little profit after he paid his stable cost and gave Uncle John a few dollars a month for renting and caring for his horse and rig. He told me to go ahead and rig Lee Ball's horse to the buggy.

JoJo drove the buggy and I took off on the mare. When JoJo got there I had already told Mr. Ford I was quitting and going to Ohio in a few days. He tried to talk me out of it. Until I began to cram my clothes and extra shoes in my canvas bag, I didn't know I had this much clothing. I had to get a big mill bag from Mrs. Ford to hold some of them while I was cleaning out the drawers.

I thought I'd better tell them the real reason I was leaving. They were really shook up when I got through telling them all the ex-sheriff had told me. I said, "I guess he's on his way out here now to warn you. He wanted to tell you instead of me."

JoJo drove the buggy up and we loaded my bags in the back. We left Mr. and Mrs. Ford standing in the yard waving good-bye.

Mr. Ford didn't care how he made a dollar, just so he made it. But they had been good to me and I would always hold them as some of the truest friends I ever had.

ELEVEN

FOR THE NEXT TWO DAYS, I went to every place in town, asking for any kind of work I could get. I went to both wholesales and the lumber yard and got promises of work at each of them to unload boxcars as they came in, starting the next week.

I knew I couldn't work at all three. H.T. Hackney being the oldest and largest, I thought I'd better take their offer. I knew all the workers there. They had two big teams of horses and big, wide wagons for delivering locally.

I told JoJo and his Mom of getting me a job, and Mrs. Walters came over and gave me a big hug. JoJo started slapping me on the back and said, "This calls for a celebration. Mom, tomorrow is Red's birthday. Let's make it a double celebration. He'll be a sweet sixteen and ain't never been kissed!"

We all got a laugh out of JoJo's ideas. I said, "It's just another day, so don't go making any plans on my account."

Mrs. Walters worked all morning in the kitchen preparing dinner. This being Sunday and JoJo not working, a large group of his friends and mine gathered under a big sprawling oak out front, pitching horseshoes and telling girl tales, some good and some dirty ones. Two of the boys had a quart of colored moonshine wrapped up, laying at the roots of the tree. They had put a few cinnamon berries in each jar and it gave the liquor a golden color and a sweet taste. Every time one of us threw a ringer, he'd get to take a snort of it. When Mrs. Walters called us to dinner, all of us were feeling our oats, laughing at each other, staggering around like a chicken with its head cut off.

I wasn't expecting anything to be different from any other Sunday dinner, but when I looked at that table piled with food my eyes nearly popped. We got seated and Mrs. Walters gave the blessings. She thanked the Lord for about everything you could think of and she started in thanking Him for looking out for me and to forgive my mother and father for the way they had treated me. Amen.

After her talk with the Lord, all us boys sobered up and started eating. Everyone tried to out-eat the other one, stuffing our bellies with all the good things before us. Then she brought a big white cake with red cinnamon berries spelling "Happy Birthday, Red." I still think that was the happiest birthday I ever had.

The local set two boxcars on the wholesale siding sometime during the night, loaded with cases of tinned foods. The shipping clerk assigned me and one more man to start unloading and stacking on the third floor. Six cases were all that could be placed on each cart, and we had 300 cases in each car. We worked two extra hours getting done. That, I think, was the hardest day's work I had ever done, but in later years that job seemed like play. I worked all summer unloading cars and filling orders to be stacked on the loading dock.

Early in the fall one of the drivers took sick and stayed off from work two weeks. Meeks, the shipping clerk, put me to driving his team, delivering around town. I sure did take a fancy to sitting up high, moving from one store to another, dropping off food of all kinds.

The ex-sheriff came up to where I was unloading my last item one day and told me Mr. Ford had passed away with a heart attack. The government agents had raided his home and confiscated over 300 gallons of moonshine. The heart attack occurred en route to the federal jail in London.

I drove the team back to the wholesale and told Meeks about it. He said, "Mr. Ford is going to be missed." Mr. Ford had gotten a contract from them for the fall and winter hauling across Pine Mountain.

I had lost a good friend. Meeks let me stay off work two days for the funeral. He knew of our close friendship. During the funeral time, Mrs. Ford said, "I'm going to sell the farm, the stock, and everything that would remind me of all the hardships and planning we have done over the years." Then she would start blowing her nose and wiping her eyes and sobbing. A big sawmilling company from Bell County bought all the horses and wagons. The other farm animals were sold to neighboring farms.

I reported for work the next morning and Meeks asked me to go to the front office. The manager wanted to see me. I couldn't think of anything I had done wrong, but I felt like I was being sent up front to be fired. I began to feel nervous.

I knocked before entering and stood there fingering my cap, trying not to appear nervous. Then Mr. Noe said, "Have a seat, Red." When he spoke like that, I let out my breath. I know my face was red. I could feel it coming back to normal.

Mr. Noe got to talking about Mr. Ford's contract. He said, "This has put the company in a bind." No one else around town had wagons or horses that could pull a good payload across the mountain. He wanted to know if I knew of a team and wagon that could do the job.

I was now getting my nervousness over and felt sorta important, him asking me for advice. He got up and poured two cups of coffee and handed me one. Then he asked if I had any suggestions.

I nodded my head and said, "I don't think you would agree." I went ahead and told him of my idea. "You should use the two largest horses of the company's and the lightest wagon, and with a good scotcher they could handle a three- to four-ton load anywhere on the mountain."

He got up and walked back and forth a few times, then he said, "That's a damn good suggestion, if you'll do the driving."

Then I got to thinking back to when Jesse had asked me about my driving and I told him my aim was to become the best. I was beginning to get a tingling feeling, to have someone like Mr. Noe asking for my opinion on something. He agreed for me to have complete charge of the two largest horses and the smaller wagon and have them rigged and shoed for mountain work. I got all this done and I got Jesse for a scotcher.

JoJo and Mrs. Walters were pleased about me being called back to the mountain. For the next few days, I worked the horses to the lighter wagon, hauling loads four and five miles, getting them to know the different commands that I would call out to them, not using the checkreins.

This Saturday evening Mr. Noe and Meeks were standing on the loading dock as I came into sight. They never took their eyes off me as I pulled in beside the dock. I called out "Ho," and them two horses put the brake on. They stopped like they had run into a brick wall. Mr. Noe asked if I had everything ready for my try at the mountain. I said, "Any time you're ready to send me, I'm ready to go."

Meeks said to back the wagon to the dock, it would be easier to load. I thought I'd smart off a little and show how I had the horses under command. While standing on the dock, I started talking to the lead horse in a low commanding tone. Then I gave the off horse a different command. They started side-stepping till I called "Ho." They stopped and I started them forward till the rear of the wagon was facing the dock and the front wheels were in line with the rear. I called "Ho" and they stopped.

I asked Meeks how close he wanted the wagon. He measured with his hands. The lead horse turned his head and looked back as if he was waiting for another command. I called each one by name and started backing them to within one foot of the dock. Meeks said, "That beats any damn thing I ever seen." He said he had noticed me talking to the horses like they were people and he thought I might be a little crazy. Mr. Noe agreed with Meeks that what they had seen would never be believed by anyone.

I left the wagon there at the dock. Meeks said, "I'll leave the invoices in the footlocker and the wagon will be loaded and ready to go by daylight Monday morning." Mr. Noe told me to be mighty careful and take my time going and coming back.

I barned the horses, rubbing them down and talking to them. I checked their feet, mouth, and eyes. They were in perfect shape. I locked the main door and went back to grease the wagon, check for loose bolts, and cover it with the canvas. It looked more like a prairie schooner than a wholesale wagon.

Meeks was letting Jesse work in the wholesale, just to hold on to him till we started our mountain trips. With everything set and planned, we left the loading dock Monday morning at dawn. Meeks had hired another man to drive his team of mules to help us on this first trip. We were loaded heavy. Meeks said we were hauling a little over four ton. The load was bulky, but it was tied down good.

Jesse was a good scotcher and kept his eyes peeled for any kind of a load shift or slackness in the lines that held the load. The big town horses, which had never been on a road as steep and rough as this, were doing a great job. On every command, they obeyed perfectly.

We made this first trip without a hitch. Every case and bag arrived at the school unscratched. Mr. Noe was very pleased about making the wholesale's first trip with their own rig and he gave Jesse and me two days off.

Jesse worked his two off days for Uncle Hamp Huff, butchering hogs. Uncle Hamp would pay him, and for a bonus he'd give him the chitlins. Now, if you don't know what chitlins are, they are the guts of a hog. I've watched colored folks prepare them from the belly of a hog to a nice clean pile of meat. They say it's a delicious dish. I only have their word, for I've never tried them.

Our trips continued through till late spring. Sometimes nothing but sugar and half-gallon fruit jars going to some little store where the moonshiners could buy what they needed to keep their businesses going.

On my off days my friends and I would loaf about town. We'd stand around street corners and drugstores that had soda fountains. I was getting sorta popular with the group I ran around with, me being the only one that always had the money for sodas and five-cent hamburgers and sometimes a hicky. A hicky was a dinner or supper plate served at the Green Parrot Pool Room and Restaurant, owned by a man that should never be forgotten by the members of the United Mine Workers' Union.

He used his pool room and restaurant for a place for all the union committeemen to meet with agents from the union headquarters, to discuss activities in their growing underground membership. He served any man, woman, or child a free hicky or bowl of soup any time they asked for it. Sometimes fifty or more would be lined around the horseshoe counter eating hickies and free soup.

A hicky plate was helpings of mashed potatoes, brown beans, a big slice of onion and chili sauce on the mashed potatoes, a patty of hamburger, or a hotdog and a bun. If you didn't have fifteen cents to pay for it, it would be free. Thousands of hungry miners have eaten free food and met with union agents behind closed doors at the Green Parrot Restaurant.

I was now seventeen years old and it seemed like I should be a lot older, as I look back and bring to mind all the times I'd been hungry and nearly frozen, sleeping in barns or on mountains, shivering and rolling around trying to stay warm. Broken away from home, with nowhere to go but wander and hope I might be welcomed at someone else's home.

The government had started a youth program called the C.C.C., the Civilian Conservation Corps. A youth had to be eighteen years old to join. Here I was, just past seventeen, the youngest of my friends that were joining up. They all told me to up my age and go in with them. I quit my job and passed my age as eighteen and enlisted in the C.C.C.

It was a great experience, going through all the training, physical examinations, and being drilled, just like army men, only we were armed with axes, saws, picks, and shovels. Some of the boys were shipped out to different states to dig ditches, work in rock quarries, build fire lanes or roads through mountain forests, and change water streams that were causing erosion.

I stayed in the C.C.C. for eighteen months, stationed near Harlan, doing hard work. We'd feed limestone boulders to a powerful crusher that crushed and sorted the different sizes of road bedding for the road over Pine Mountain to the settlement school. I developed a strong body and was learning to do many different kinds of work.

On my loafing days around town I often had someone to tell me how the family was doing. Dad's health was failing and my younger brothers and my sisters were doing poorly. Jim and Amos had left the mountain and gone back to work in the coal mines. Dad had sold the big blacks. The farm was run down and no one was there to keep things going. I made an allotment to Mom of twenty-five dollars a month from the pay of my service to the C.C.C., keeping five dollars each month for myself. I supplemented my five dollars by setting up a camp barbershop, using only a nailed stool, a pocket comb, and a sixty-cent pair of hair scissors. I used an old torn sheet the supply clerk furnished for a barber cloth.

Twice a week we were allowed to visit a town or some nearby farm for an evening or weekend. I had met Mae, the girl that was later to be my wife (and still is), before I joined the C.C.C. I would always manage to have enough money to get a few beers and get Mae tuned up to go to a movie, not looking at the movie, just sitting there holding hands, hugging and kissing, when the big picture screen didn't have the sitting area all lit up.

Mae was a country gal, raised over across Pine Mountain in Letcher County, back in the woods where you had to swing out on grapevines or climb cliffs to get out. She had come to Harlan, living with one of her older brothers that had swung out earlier and come to Harlan and married Uncle Hamp Huff's niece. Mae wanted to get an education and a husband, and I became the victim. But I've enjoyed being her victim. By being stationed near the town of Harlan I could sorta be around and keep the wolves from her, trying to keep her interested in me.

After my discharge from the C.C.C., I knocked around town for a while, staying at Mrs. Walters'. JoJo had left for the big cities. The coal mines were working nearly every day but mine owners had cut their pay below half of what the company union had bargained for. They had rehired meaner and more gun thugs to force the miners to work. All the promises that were made to get them to break away from the U.M.W. of A. and join the company union were ignored, and violence and killings of nonagreeable miners were being committed all over the county.

The federal government was still shipping food to needy families. I thought of what all the miners had gone through before, and here it was happening again. Every store in town put big signs in their windows and on the doors, stating in large letters, "All items are sold only for cash. Absolutely no credit. Please do not ask."

The welfare office would allow a miner that worked every day in the mines and couldn't make enough to feed his family to receive enough government food to keep his family from starving. A bunch of thugs would stop them and stomp on and pour out all the food they had stood in long lines to get. Then, with threats and sometimes a beating, the miner would return to work.

The new sheriff that had made all the promises to the miners was importing thugs from out of state and placing them all over the county. This is what gave Harlan its name, "Bloody Harlan." It was known by that name all over these United States of America. The sheriff was the king of all murderers. He would visit state penitentiaries and the wardens would let him pick the criminals he wanted to take back to Harlan. He would coach these criminals in the manner the mine owners wanted them to serve.

My brother Jim was working for a coal company at Kitts, Kentucky. Near 300 men worked there. The company was family-owned. Bryan Whitfield, one of the owners, was president of the company and superintendent of the mine. His brother Agustus was general manager and camp boss. The Whitfield family had broken away from the sheriff and his thugs and were doing their own policing. When the price of coal went down on the market they would post on the daily bulletin board what effect it had on the hourly rate of pay and the price they would pay per ton for loading coal. The cost of food at their company store would drop prices accordingly. No one was forced to work nor any threats made.

Jim saw me in town and asked me if I would like to work in the mine. I had been thinking about bucking against the thugs, joining the U.M.W. of A. and taking a few shots at them, but not working in the mines. He told me the Whitfield family was good to all the men and treated them all alike and he could get me a job. I thanked him and said "No."

This was the first I had seen of Jim since I left the C.C.C. I was broke, not a cent in my pocket. I had tried to get work everywhere, on farms and log woods. I even tried to get JoJo's old job. The road was finished across Pine Mountain and trucks were hauling goods over it. Nobody used horses and wagons any more except for farm work.

Amos was working for the only coal company that worked under a U.M.W. of A. contract. I decided I'd go see him and Artie. I hadn't seen them for over a year.

I loaded a canvas bag with the best of my clothes and told Mrs. Walters what I intended to do. She handed me a five-dollar bill and told me I would always be welcomed any time I wanted to come back. I kissed her cheek and left.

TWELVE

THE COMPANY Amos worked for gave me a job loading coal, and I joined the union. The company store issued all the tools that were needed. Then you paid for them after you started work. Looking at that pile of tools made sweat pop out on me. I thought that it would take me a year to load enough coal to pay for them. I had thought a pick and shovel were all you needed. There must have been twenty different tools there.

Artie and Amos were glad I'd come to live with them. They lived about fifteen miles from the mines. Amos had bought a car to ride back and forth to work.

I had no experience mining and the foreman started me off working with Amos. The pay under the union here was a lot more than the scab mines in the upper part of Harlan.

The work was hard but I was enjoying doing it. Amos would be fagged out every evening. He'd take a bath, eat his supper, then lay around till bedtime. Usually I would walk down to the near village and play a few games of pool. A lot of times I'd win more money than I'd made loading coal all day. I'm still good at eight ball.

I started missing my gal, wishing I could have got a job closer to town. I wasn't worried about her being lonesome. There were plenty of wolves around town wanting to flirt with her. I decided if I didn't want to lose her I'd better do something about it. I told Artie I was going back to Harlan and get married. I'd got a letter, the only one Mae had written me, the day before, and honey was dripping from the envelope it was so sweet.

The next day I went to the mine office and got a settlement of wages due me. It amounted to $9. Train fare to Harlan cost fifty cents. I went to see my girl and talked her into a quick marriage. The marriage license cost $5 and I gave the preacher $3. That left me with fifty cents, a new bride, no home, and no job.

We spent our honeymoon night at my wife's brother's, where she was making her home. The next morning, after she had prepared me a breakfast, I made up my mind that I now had a responsibility and had to do something about it. The mines were working good, but the workers had to get government aid to live on and I wasn't about to go on welfare or work in a scab mine if I could help it.

I had the fifty cents left over from my marriage. I bought twenty-five cents' worth of cheese, headed for Loyall railroad yards, and caught a freight to the Corbin yards. After eating about a third of my cheese while the train was coming to a stop, choking it down without anything to drink, I peeped through a crack in the door and saw two men unloading a boxcar of lumber into a large truck.

I slid the door open enough to jump out and ran back to where the two men were working. I watched them moving the lumber clumsy-like, not taking advantage of their effort. I asked the older one if he could use any help handling that lumber. If he could, I said, I'd had a lot of experience loading and unloading lumber.

He said, "Hop up here, you got a job, if you'll help unload this car for a dollar."

I climbed up in the truck. They had loaded three bundles of ship-lap boards, each bundle weighing about a hundred pounds. I looked at the different lengths and sizes of the bundles and told the older man we could load it in the truck without carrying it. He said, "How in the hell can you do that?"

I scooted a short square bundle of lumber to the center of the door and told the older man to stay in the truck. The other man went to the rear of the car, then I laid the end of a bundle of ship-lap on top of the square bundle. The man in the rear raised the other end and started sliding the bundle to the man in the truck. As he slid the bundle, I went to the rear of the car, the older man guiding the bundle to where he wanted it. The other man, pushing it to the edge of the flat bundle, would lay this end in line with the truck bed. The man working with me would lay the end of another bundle atop of the sliding bundle and I would start pushing it to the older man. We kept going like this till the truck was loaded full, without stopping.

The old man said, "Where in the hell did you learn to handle lumber like that? That's the easiest and fastest I ever seen that much lumber loaded!"

I told him us folks further up in the mountains made do with what we had to do with. We hauled two loads to a big barn, to be slid and stacked at the rear of the truck, with them sliding and me guiding and stacking.

We went for another load. We stopped at a little store to get something to eat. I spent my last quarter for a big round pineapple-filled tart with a lot of powdered sugar icing all over it and a quart of sweet milk. With this, and about half of my cheese, I had a good lunch.

It took three more loads to empty the car. The older man said he'd give me a dollar and a half a day if I wanted to work for him.

I told him I had just gotten married and was looking for a job to earn enough money to support me and my wife and I couldn't do it on a dollar and a half a day. He handed me a dollar and said, "Here's another fifty cents for teaching me how to handle lumber."

I walked back to the little store and bought me another tart and a quart of milk, then hurried back to the railroad yard. A big mally was making up steam on the Ohio line. I darted from car to car as the train started easing out. Finally, finding a car not sealed, I slid the door open, jumped in, and closed the door. A voice came from the rear of the car, welcoming me to ride in his car.

I felt my way back to where the voice came from and hunkered down beside the man. He told me he had been bumming around from state to state for the past five years and had enjoyed doing it. He said, "I don't have a damn worry in the world and mean to do it as long as I live, or as long as I can climb in a boxcar."

The train picked up speed as we sat there in the darkness. While he was telling me all about himself, we opened the door and sat with our legs hanging out, looking at farm after farm. As we traveled through the rolling hills, he asked me about myself. I told him I was headed for Ohio to hunt work, that I had just gotten married and had no place to take my wife, except maybe to a scab coal mine and both of us starve. I then brought out my food and shared it with him. As the train slowed down coming into Decoursey yards, he started telling me about all the different states and cities he'd been in. His aim was to hobo through all the others. I got him to agree to go with me to the transit house. He'd never been there. He said, "I don't like to have people ordering me around."

He wore new looking overalls, a nice black jacket, and he had his boots shined like glass. If you saw him on the street you'd never think he was a hobo. My clothes were fairly clean and I'd pass for just an ordinary person. We walked from Decoursey to the transit house. The same lady was still at the desk. We filled out the cards she handed us and were shown to our bunks. We got to eat supper before we bathed.

The next morning a note was laying on my clothes telling me my friend had left during the night. It stated that he couldn't lay around in a place like this and was moving on. He wished me luck in finding a job and hoped to see me in the future.

I would start every morning, just after breakfast, and walk from place to place trying to find a job. Sometimes there would be over a hundred men lined up filling out job application blanks for only one opening. It was like this at every job site or factory I went to. There just wasn't any job to be found. The lady at the desk assigned me to another floor and five more days of free food and a bunk. She said, "I know you are trying to find work and I will cover for you."

I thanked her and kept walking the streets day after day. "No Help Wanted" was posted at the entrance gates at nearly every job site I went to.

I had given up and was planning to go back to the mountains the next morning. As I was making my way back to the transit house I had a streak of luck. I walked into a job. A big restaurant was changing furniture and kitchen fixtures, and paying $2 a day for ten hours' work. I told the lady at the transit house desk about getting the job, and how much money I was to get. She said, "You can stay here while you are doing the job, but you are to make a contribution from your earnings to the transit house. You can pay it at my desk."

I still had seventy-five cents I had earned in Corbin, three silver quarters. I was holding onto them. In case I got hungry going back to Harlan, I could get me some cheese and crackers.

I worked at the changeover for the restaurant nine days and learned a lot from the old man that was in charge of the work. He told me if I decided to stay in Cincinnati I could work for him regular for the same wages I was making now. I told him I had married and didn't see how I could make it on $2 a day in the city. He didn't like it, me not accepting his offer. He paid me off and said that was all the work he needed from me.

I gave the lady at the transit house $4 and bought me a ticket to Harlan at the Greyhound bus station. I was going back in style, with a new pair of shoes, overalls, shirt, and black leather cap.

When I got to Harlan I still had $4 and a dime. I had won $3.50 rolling dice in the rear of the bus. I'd talk to them dice like they understood every word I was saying. Like, "Come on seven, I'm on my way to heaven," or "Little Joe from Kokomo," sometimes calling on eleven, and saying, "I'm still on my way to heaven." That sure made the ride back to Harlan pass fast.

I'd been gone from Harlan twenty-seven days. Mae was living at her brother's and working in a little restaurant he had opened up named the Little Daisy. She ran the front and her sister-in-law ran the kitchen. I stopped in the restaurant to say hello to Mae and to ask her if she remembered her husband. She sure gave me a cold-shoulder look. When she got a chance, she came to where I was sitting and wanted to know where I'd been.

I never told her why I left or where I'd been, until now. The only reason I've told her about it is because she is helping me with spelling the difficult words beyond my ability.

I got back in good graces with Mae and she decided to go back across Pine Mountain to live with her father and stepmother while I hunted a job and got a place to bring her to live.

I got a job with the Blue Diamond Coal Company installing mining fans, earning $2.40 a day. I stayed at Mrs. Walters' for three weeks, walking across a big mountain to and from work, about five miles each way, not spending anything except buying a little something for my lunch and giving Mrs. Walters $3 a week for my board and laundry.

A lady I knew, Mrs. High, who lived alone in a big house, and I ask her if she would let me pay her $5 a week for a bedroom and the use of her kitchen. I told her I had married and didn't have a place to live but I had a good job and enough money to pay two weeks' rent.

She showed me the bedroom and the kitchen and said we could use the living room for that much money. I paid her $10 and went to an A & P store and bought a supply of food to last two weeks. I had $14 left. I got a friend to drive his car, a 1920 Whippet Overland, across Pine Mountain on the road the C.C.C. had built.

Mae acted like she didn't care whether she came back with me or not. I thought for a while I'd made all these preparations for nothing. I learned later she and one of her past boyfriends had been planning for her to get an annulment of our marriage and for them to wed. She packed a few things in a box and said she would go with me and try to get herself settled.

Mrs. High welcomed her to the house. She said, "I have known Red all my life." I think she wanted to tell Mae about what she knew about my family and me. I shook my head for her not to say anything further and she hushed. I had never told Mae about that, either.

Mae liked the kitchen and the room. She prepared a supper and invited Mrs. High to eat with us. She accepted the offer. After the supper we went to a movie and visited a little grocery store on our way back for a few things I had failed to get at the A & P store, such as black pepper, soap, writing paper, and a bottle of catsup. Now ain't that a hell of a thing for a fellow to remember? But to me it seems like it was just yesterday it happened.

I made contact with a man living at Loyall, a little railroad town below Harlan. He agreed to let me ride to and from work for a dollar a week, a distance of sixteen miles there and back. Mae seemed like she was accepting this way of living. She would some days visit her brother in Harlan while I was at work.

I tried to please her every time I got a chance by plucking big snowball flowers and summer roses from a house up the street. Forming a large bouquet, she would place them in a tall drinking glass of water, keeping them fresh for several days. Some evenings I'd stop at a little store and get a cup or two of ice cream or something else to please her, trying to win back her affections.

I was working hard every day, but after the coal company got through holding part of my pay for what was called cuts, there wasn't but very little left to pay rent and buy groceries. We were just barely getting by, but I was happy having my wife with me and I vowed to myself that I would never stop trying to keep her happy or providing for her.

One evening I came home to our rented apartment and no one was there. Mrs. High came from down the street, where she had been visiting a neighbor, and told me that my Mom had come earlier and talked my wife into going on the mountain to live with them. Mae, not knowing anything about why I'd never stayed at home, went with her.

I thanked Mrs. High and took off for the mountain. I said, "I might be back. I can't understand why they wanted her up there."

They had told me to never come back, and here I was, climbing the mountain, getting mad as hell every step I took. Why in the hell couldn't they let their woods colt alone and mind their own business? This was running through my mind all the way up the mountain.

I finally reached the house, after stopping several times, cussing myself for being me, wishing I was somebody else and was ten thousand miles away from anybody I knew. Mom and Dad were sitting

112

on the porch watching me as I came into the yard. I couldn't bring myself to speak first. I stood there waiting for one of them to say something.

When Mae came through the door with a big smile on her face, I knew they had buttered up to her with a lot of sweet talk, telling her what a great family they were. They hadn't told her about trying to pawn me off to different people when I was between the ages of six and nine years, and then later running me off and telling me to never come back. I was thinking this as I stood there looking at Mae, with the big smile on her face, coming towards me.

I sat on the edge of the porch, waiting for someone to say something about why Mom had talked Mae into coming here. I was about to tell Mae to get our clothes and return to Mrs. High's, when Mom said, "I thought it best if you stayed here and saved a few paychecks to pay down on some furniture. I thought I owed you that much for the way you helped before, and I used all the money you sent me from the government while you was in the C.C.C." She didn't mention all the money they got while I was working the big blacks for the coal company, or what they got for them when they sold them.

Mae seemed to be happy among them. Taking me by the arm, she led me into the house. I had promised myself many times that I would never enter their home again. Mae had helped cook supper and had fixed a favorite dish or two of mine, knowing I'd be hungry after a day's work and a climb up the mountain.

All the family seated themselves at their favorite seats and settled, eating a quiet supper. There wasn't very much talk during supper. I had been very hungry when I sat down to eat, but now I felt like I would choke if I ate a bite. I couldn't bring myself to relax. I tried to act like I had accepted their offer for us to stay there, all the time cussing myself for it. I should have got Mae by the arm and stormed off that mountain, but I didn't. I managed to hold myself in control, but it was one of the hardest decisions I had ever made.

We stayed on the mountain for two weeks. Every evening I would go to the company office, trying to get them to rent me a camp house. I didn't care if we had any furniture or not. I could easily throw up a makeshift bed and we could cook in the open fireplace. I would have been willing to live under a cliff, just to get me and Mae away from there.

On this Friday evening I went to the office to see if a house had become empty and the bookkeeper told me I could have one they controlled at a worked-out mine between there and Harlan. I signed for it. I didn't care what kind of shape it was in, just so it was a house.

When I got to the mountain and told Mae, she was thrilled over getting the house. We started counting what few dollars we had and the amount of pay due me at the mine office.

Mae went off the mountain to town that evening to buy some things for her kitchen. There was a five and ten cent store, J.J. Newberry, that stocked about everything you could think of. Mae had $6. She bought enough pots and pans and dishes for us to make out on for a little over $4.

The next day, Saturday, we rode a bus to Gray's Knob, the worked-out coal mine that leased their camp houses to the company I was working for, to scrub and clean our house. It was a large, square, four-room house. The front entrance was the kitchen door. A community well pump was near the end of the porch. The privacy with a two-hole seat was in the back. The house had an open fireplace in each bedroom and an electric light overhead in each room. We scrubbed the two front rooms and cleaned the walls and windows. They sure were dirty. The people who had lived there before must have lived like pigs. But we scrubbed the floors and washed the walls till they looked like new.

Mae and I planned the things she was to get at the company store. They stocked every kind of furniture a miner needed to keep house with. When a new worker had proven he was a reliable everyday worker, he could get about anything he needed to live on, and the bookkeeper would deduct from his pay so much each week.

Mae picked a nice bedroom suit, a big high-back cane rocker to rock the baby that was soon to come, a kitchen cookstove with a warming closet, a dinette set, a big wide kitchen cabinet, and a linoleum for the kitchen floor. She got everything we needed to set up housekeeping with for $147. The company store delivery man helped Mae arrange the furniture in two of the rooms. She also got a big supply of staple groceries and fresh foods to last for a month. When I came from work Mae had a good supper waiting for me, with a big smile on her face to go with it.

Cold weather was starting, snow flurries coming, with the strong winds blowing it against the window pane. The snow would stick to the warm glass, which caused it to melt and freeze, then stack up to several inches thick. But we were warm, with a big roaring open fire ablaze day and night.

I worked every day, paying a goodly sum each week on our fur-

114

niture, and soon got it paid down to where the store manager let me add a small radio to the remaining debt. Mae sure acted like she was pleased with it. She said, "I didn't have a soul to speak to until you'd come in from work." Except the baby that kept moving and kicking around in her belly.

My brother Jim got a better job at another mine, located further up Martin's Fork than where I worked, and the company he had worked for forced him to move from their camp. I let him move his furniture in and live in the other two rooms of our house. His wife was soon to give birth to their second child. The first one, Billy Nick, was petted on by everyone who saw him.

After Jim and his family got settled in and he started working at his new job, he and I got to be together every evening. We never discussed what had happened on the mountain. We talked of mining and how we used to nearly freeze on the wagon trips over Pine Mountain. Sometimes we'd mention something about the killings and rapes that had been done during the long coal strikes by the Kentucky state military and the company-hired thugs.

The winter was really setting in. It would come a hard rain, sometimes lasting all day. Then at night, as it got colder, it would turn to sleet. All the roads and streets throughout the county would become a sheet of ice. When you thought the next day would bring a little warmth it would start snowing and the strong winds would blow the snow with howling force and pile it in drifts four to six feet high. The whole county would be crippled from the storm until a warm sun and gentle breeze would melt the snow. The frozen rivers and streams would melt and cause floods that undermined roads along the rivers and streams, causing them to collapse, stopping any help to the many families that would need medical aid or food. With nearly all the power lines down, electric-powered coal mines would have to sit idle for several days while crews trudged over mountains repairing broken cables and bracing up fallen power poles.

Christmas was coming near. Mae and I were very willing to let it pass without expecting anything from each other. We spent the day quietly in our two rooms. Sometimes Billy Nick would come bursting through the door we kept unlocked between our separate rooms with some kind of a winding toy for me to fix or look at.

The repairs were made and work at the mines was getting under-way. It looked like the weather was calming down, until New Year's Eve. It started again, worse than the one everybody had come from under just a few days past. It would rain, then freeze. Snow would come, then sleet, then more snow. When you tried to walk in it you would break through the crust of ice underneath the top layer of snow.

It was like that when Mae started having a bellyache. She started walking back and forth from the kitchen to the bedroom, moaning and groaning, with tears in her eyes and a scared look on her face. She kept this up for over an hour. Finally she said I'd better go for the doctor.

I geared myself for the coldness outside. George Douglas, who lived directly behind my house, owned a 1926 Buick and kept tire chains on nearly all the time. Any time there was an emergency, he was called on. I waded snow and ice to George's house and called him to the door. I told him I had to get a doctor, for Mae was having our baby. He grabbed a coat and came out in a hurry and said, "Let's go!" We left that camp like we were being shot at. The rear wheels were throwing snow and ice ten feet in the air.

We went to the coal company doctor's house. He was on another granny race and wouldn't be back till after midnight. So George and I headed for Harlan Hospital for another doctor. The only doctor at the hospital had a man on the operating table, trying to save his life. He had been brought there with frozen feet and hands.

George suggested we go to Dr. Park's home next. I was getting scared Mae would be getting worse. I said, "Let's hurry!" We had already been looking for a doctor for over two hours.

We rushed to Dr. Park's home. I could see him through the big living room windows, sitting comfortably, reading a paper. I knocked. When he came to the door, I told him about not being able to get our company doctor and asked would he go with me to aid Mae with the birth.

Dr. Park said, "This being the first baby, it's probably false pains."

I said, "I don't think so. She was in too much pain for it to be false. You'd better come with me. If you don't go to deliver her baby and anything happens to my wife, I'm coming back to see you."

He must have seen the determined look on my face. He got his little black bag and said, "You ride with me."

Very little talk was done as we followed George back. We stomped the snow off our boots and went into the kitchen. Mrs. Allen, a neighbor across the street, came over. When she heard Dr. Park's car drive up she knew what was happening and wanted to be of some help. The doctor hurried and examined Mae. He said, "We're going to have the baby here in a few minutes."

It wasn't over two or three minutes till I heard the baby cry. Dr. Park said, "I'm glad you insisted I come. She would have had trouble without my help."

I offered to follow the doctor back to Harlan, with George in the big Buick. I was afraid he might get stalled in the snow and ice, but he thought he could make it without chains.

THIRTEEN

BILL WAS A FINE, HEALTHY BABY, perfect in form and very pretty. It didn't take long for me to learn the effect of closeness to him. He seemed to want to snuggle up to me more than he did to his mother.

Winter was over and the county work crews and the W.P.A. workers were busy cleaning up road ditches and hauling rock and gravel from river banks to fill in big holes rutted out in all the roads. The coal mines were working about every day. Things were running along smoothly.

Mae and I decided we wanted to move into the camp where I worked. The foreman on my shift was having me stay late three and four evenings a week. I was having difficulty getting home, a distance of six miles, some evenings having to walk it and maybe getting caught in a hard rain and no shelter along the road but big trees.

I started checking with the office every evening for a house closer to work. Finally they rented me one up near the mine. I could walk to and from the mine in less than five minutes.

The house was about two miles up the hollow from the company store. My foreman put me to working on the night shift and Mae would enjoy walking with some of the neighboring women to the store. They did their gossiping as they went to and from it, toting bags of groceries.

I had a lot of idle time during the day, nothing to do but look out the back, up the mountain, and watch mining locomotives go back and forth with long lines of loaded cars of coal, or look out the front, which faced a larger mountain that at one time had had a farm.

Mae soon got with child again, with nothing else for us to do or much to talk about. I didn't have anything to do but work at night and sleep all day. I was beginning to think I was a bother to Mae, petting Bill and trying to teach him to say words all day, and spoiling him till she couldn't control him. She seemed glad for me to be away from the house for a while.

One morning, sitting on the front porch, looking at the big cleared fields on the mountain, I told Mae I was going to lease it and raise a crop of corn and other vegetables. Me having a lot of time in the daytime, and her already pregnant and nothing else to do, I might as well do some farming. She agreed readily.

The company I worked for owned the old hillside farm. They told me to use all of it I wanted. The land was so steep, you had to dig out a place to stand. If you missed a footing, you'd slide to the bottom and then have to climb back up. That was sure hard farming, but I managed to raise a good crop of about everything you could want. Mae canned a lot and dried a lot and I sold some and gave a lot to families that couldn't pay for it.

Our second child was born when I first started cleaning the growth of weeds and briars from the fields. She was the prettiest baby I had ever seen. We named her after two of my favorite movie stars, Norma Shearer and Jean Harlow.

The way my family was increasing, and the small wages I was making, I started planning for future foods. Mae's father gave her a young milk cow. I traded a lot of vegetables I had grown to a friend for a brood sow. I had grown enough corn to raise and fatten eight or ten pigs and still have enough to feed the milk cow all winter. The sow had ten pigs, all colored just like her. They grew fast and soon started eating. I penned the sow for fattening when she weaned the pigs. She was a big frame hog and when I butchered her she weighed near 600 pounds.

Miners all around me would go to Harlan and stand in line for a government hand-out of free food. Some of them would miss a day's work just to go and get it. Mae and I had done our planning well. We didn't have any money but we had plenty to eat.

The coal mines slowed down to two or three days' work a week. More people started signing up for government aid. The bookkeepers kept putting notices on the daily bulletin board that, as of today, the company was forced to lower the wage rate. The employees that couldn't accept the cut in pay would be asked to vacate the house they were living in so a willing worker could move in.

When John L. Lewis heard this, he did the moving in. He had William Turnblazer set up a United Mine Workers' headquarters in Harlan and start recruiting organizers for a final drive to establish a lasting union. The organizers for the miners of Harlan County, to mention a few, were George Gilbert, Ed Bean, Bob Hodge, and many dozens more of the bravest men and truest friends the miners ever had.

During the first of the slowdown of the mines, Mae got pregnant again. It seemed like every time work got slack or bad weather kept the mines shut down, about nine months from then there would be a bumper crop of babies born. Some of the babies would be called such names as "Off Day Bratt," "Slack Work Sonny," "Bad Weather Dream," "Idle John," and several more.

The organizers were going to every camp in Harlan County, signing miners up to join in the union. Some of the older men remembered the struggle in the past and feared the gun thugs and military that were sure to be used against them if they rejoined the union.

The Reverend William Clontz and Bob Hodge, organizers for the union disguised as ragged miners, visited me. They told me that George Titler, their chief, had sent them to discuss ways to bring a majority of the miners where I worked to a big rally to be held at Smith, Kentucky. It was supposed to be a secret. They gave me some money to give out to the miners for bus fare. Between then and Saturday night I saw and talked to every selected miner in our camp and gave each one bus fare to and from Smith.

There must have been ten or twelve thousand miners gathered to hear some of the greatest speeches that were ever spoken to an assembly of miners. They were eager to hear of a way to organize themselves and build a strong union. The Reverend William Clontz opened the meeting with a long, thankful prayer, asking the Lord to guide the thousands of miners under his voice to a better promise of tomorrow and to help them to overcome any opposition to organize themselves and give each man a means to protect himself against the thugs and military that would be sure to rise against them. Brother Clontz called on the Lord for a good fifteen minutes. He was applauded for about that long also.

After each speaker had delivered his speech and Brother Clontz closed with a prayer, several names were called out to remain after all the others had left. My name was called first. The men who stayed were given instructions how to carry out orders and try to maintain peace with the mine operators. Violence was to be used only to protect ourselves and we were not to allow damage to be done to company property.

The selected miners were to be talked to. We were to try to explain to them that we needed them to join our union to make us stronger in rank and help us get a better wage for our hard work. We were to explain to them that we would get aid from the northern unions and support from all the other unions through the whole United States. Our local unions would see that all members got food, clothing, and medical care for as long as it took to gain our aim.

After I visited with the opposing miners I had all of them signed into the union, one hundred percent. I turned my recorder book in to the union headquarters. George Titler, our secretary and treasurer, didn't believe I had done it and still stayed alive!

My second son, G.C., Junior (Buck), had been born in November. I started feeling a proudness building up in me because I had never asked help or aid or borrowed anything in my life. I had bought a few things on credit, but it was hard to sleep at night, thinking about owing for them. When Buck came along we had plenty of stored-up canned foods, a good milk cow, hens, and two big butchered hogs hanging in a little smokehouse I had built from sawmill slabs. I had all this, but I didn't have a dollar in cash to my name.

On the day I was notified by secret to call the miners to strike, the company bookkeeper had put the work sign in the office window, announcing work for tomorrow. On idle days miners loafed around the office and company store, just to be away from their nagging wives. Also, we'd learn news of the union that would be passed by someone who had made a trip to Harlan for some reason or other. The main reason for making a trip was to meet secretly with one of our disguised organizers and get instructions to be secretly passed to the idle miners. On this day, John L. Lewis had ordered every member in Harlan County that had joined the union to stop work and report to the elected leaders for instructions.

The next morning at our mine not a man reported for work. At eight o'clock every miner employed by this mine assembled in the big parking lot at the company store to show force to the company officials and to chant "No work" until a contract was made with our union. The superintendent of the company, Charley Burnett, asked to speak to their leaders. Me and three elected committeemen stepped forth. When Mr. Burnett saw me in the lead he seemed surprised. He said, "I thought you would be the last one of my employees to go against the company."

When he said this, the men gave me their support with a roaring approval of my leadership. Mr. Burnett asked me and the committee to join him in the office. I asked the members if I had approval to meet with him. They started yelling, "You're our leader, do what you please, but don't take no bulling from him or his thugs. We'll wait here till you give us further orders."

We then followed the superintendent into the office. We were seated at a long committee table and offered something to drink. Each of us declined the offer. Mr. Burnett seated himself at the end of the table, and Mr. Yates, the bookkeeper, was at his left with a long sheet of paper and a pencil to take notes with. His thug, Joe Morris, was sitting at his right.

Mr. Burnett being a well educated man, I knew he would use his knowledge to gain any information he could from us. Me with a very limited knowledge of big words and their meanings, had asked for my good friend James Bodie to be elected to the committee to help me understand statements made at any meeting we were to attend. When the superintendent started telling me how good the company had always treated its employees, my friend and committeeman would give me the meaning of the statement, or tell me if a certain word had a different meaning.

Mr. Burnett was making big talk about what would happen if the miners refused to listen to their employer instead of some bushy-browed Russian Red who was using the hard-working miners of America to furnish him with funds to set up big business and factories in Russia and other foreign countries. He called the members of the union John L. Lewis puppets.

James Bodie stood up and told the superintendent, "We have had enough of your insults and name calling." He looked to me to give our departing words.

I told Mr. Burnett, "We are starting, as of today, a cease-work program throughout all the bituminous coal fields until each coal company has accepted an agreement with the United Mine Workers' Union of America. We have the support of all the anthracite coal fields to go along with us. We intend to stay on a peaceful strike as long as it takes for you and others like you to recognize their employees and sign a contract that will be drawn up with them and our parent union."

I told him, "The first thing the men from this company want you to do is to get rid of your two thugs and take down your 'Work Tomorrow' sign and, to show you have some care for your employees, to let them remain living in your houses, and allow each miner one dollar a day in company scrip to be spent in your store.

"For this, we, the committee, will allow you to use a rotating crew of our union members to keep pumps running and slate falls cleaned up. These men will be paid at the scale you're paying now. If you can't agree to this, please don't attempt to operate your mines. No one can tell what might happen if either side of this work stoppage erupts into violence or if any attempt is made to operate any coal mine. Our orders are to be peaceful and cooperative with all the mine operators.

"Now, if you'll excuse me and my party, we'll wait outside while you decide on this matter. We thank you."

As we passed him in going out he had a blank expression on his face and his lips were quivering, like he was trying to say something and couldn't get it out.

All the men we had left in the parking area were still waiting to learn how the meeting turned out. I told them I had laid it on the line, just like we had voted on, and now we were waiting for him to decide.

Most of the men settled into small groups, talking of the many days that might be spent loafing, fishing, hunting, and mainly just waiting for a contract to work under. Others would start a card game or roll dice for matches. No one had any money to gamble with.

After about an hour, Mr. Yates, the bookkeeper, appeared and called for the committee to come to the office. As we came to the door, Joe Morris was coming through without his guns and badge.

Mr. Yates asked us to be seated and offered us another drink, which we refused again. Mr. Burnett was sitting there where we had left him and still had the blank look on his face. He hadn't expected any one of his employees to stand up against him. He asked if we cared for a smoke. We all accepted a cigarette.

As we lit up, Yates began telling of the decision he and the superintendent had made by phone to company headquarters in Knoxville, Tennessee. JoJo Bonnyman, the president of the Blue Diamond Coal Company, had given the superintendent orders to agree with what the committee had asked for until further notice and do it respectfully to all the men at this mine.

I noticed the two big guns laying on the table where the thug had been sitting. Mr. Burnett saw me staring at them and told Yates to put them away. He asked me how many men he could have to keep the mines in order. I told him as many as he needed, but the crews would be rotated each day. I was to have a list of the different tasks each man was to do, and would furnish him a man capable of doing each job.

I said, "You can direct the men I send to do any kind of maintenance work to keep the mines free of water and slate falls but not have them do anything in the line of producing coal."

Bodie said, "Give him a list of what he can have them do and what he can't have them do."

The superintendent agreed to that. We thanked them for their cooperation and Yates said he would send me a list each evening of what the superintendent wanted done the next day.

Outside in the parking lot the men came to meet us. Bodie started telling what had happened inside the office. The men started applauding their approval. Bodie told them a system would be set up at his house each Friday, notifying them what crews were to report to the mines the following week. Bodie, the only one of the committee owning a car, furnished us transportation.

We drove to Harlan to report to headquarters that all our requests had been granted and that Joe Morris, the thug, had been fired and told to leave the camp.

George Titler, our leader and instructor on how to handle any union affairs, said, "This calls for a celebration." He brought out a bottle and passed it around, with a lot of handshaking and laughter over how we had handled our assignment.

We then got down to the future things that had to be done to keep the thousands of idle miners happy. Distribution centers for food had to be planned, and men to be in charge of issuing the food would be chosen at each camp. Local trucks had to be hired to deliver to the many camps. A large warehouse was rented to us by the lumber yard people; their business was dead, nobody had any money to build. People over the county were either on government aid or waiting to draw union aid.

George Titler announced that food and medical aid for all members of the union were now available and trucks would start this day to deliver food to each coal camp and other places selected, to distribute to all the union members.

In each local union, men would load a fleet of trucks willingly to rush the food to waiting members in distant coal camps who were in bad need of it. Most of the companies refused to allow their striking employees to have credit of one dollar a day. A lot of them re-

124

fused to discharge their thugs, saying they feared for the safety of their supervisors and themselves. They reported to the sheriff's office threats and dynamite bombs being blasted in their coal tipples causing thousands of dollars of damage. They asked the sheriff to furnish them protection with more thugs to insure safety for willing workers they had gotten to work in the mine.

The mine owners sent team after team of hiring agents to Alabama, Ohio, and Illinois with promises of great riches, or any other kind of promises, just to get people there to migrate to Harlan and work as strikebreakers. We called them scabs. Most of them had never seen the inside of a coal mine.

The sheriff of Harlan, when he was first elected, was thought to be one of the most honest persons that had ever asked to be elected to a county office. He started out by firing all the deputies the outgoing sheriff had left for him. The people that voted for him thought that was the greatest thing he could have done. He then started hiring local men, dressing them in neat uniforms, each one wearing a steel breast plate and a shiny new gun on each hip, slung low and tied down. These men were to be the most fearless and honest men to be found in Harlan County. There wasn't to be any more fee grabbing. Arrests were to be made without beatings and abuse.

This changed soon, when the sheriff started having great sums of money and partnerships in some of the mines given to him. Each two of his deputies were given a new Ford car, with bulletproof glass, to patrol the roads and the coal camps that housed the brought-in scabs from other states.

It wasn't long before the first mine started working with a few of our union backsliders and hundreds of untrained strikebreakers. Guarding them were the uniformed sheriff's deputies, each armed with an automatic shotgun, and some with high-powered rifles. Soon other mines posted work signs on their bulletin boards after they had moved in scab labor and had promises from the sheriff of his protection against the striking miners.

R.C. Tway was the second company to start work. We had sent many truckloads of good food to be issued to the members of our union living in the camp. Several sick cases had been admitted to the Harlan Hospital and the bill was sent to our secretary and treasurer to be paid. Nearly every man living at R.C. Tway reported for work.

When the news of the companies bringing in out-of-state strikebreakers, and of the sheriff's deputies rampaging through the county, reached John L. Lewis in Washington, he got the ball rolling. If the coal companies thought the strikes were hard to break before, they would have one hell of a time stopping us now. If they thought their deputy sheriffs were fearless, they hadn't seen nothing yet. Thousands and thousands of union coal miners from neighboring counties rolled into Harlan armed with any kind of weapon they could get. Groups of leaders gathered at our headquarters to be briefed on their assignments.

More hordes of union miners giving us their support were coming in over the mountains from Virginia and West Virginia. They swept from camp to camp, forcing the strikebreakers and deputies to flee. They set fires to many buildings being used to house the scabs and thugs. There were many thousands of angry miners roaming through the mountains seeking vengeance against scabs, gun thugs, and mine owners. Mine owners' property was being destroyed for having worked the men at starvation wages.

We knew we had to get in a lot of licks before troops were sent in. Trains leaving Harlan were loaded to full capacity for over a week with fleeing scabs. Hardly any of them had families with them. They just grabbed their other shirt and fled.

With none of the mines attempting to work, a group of union strikers decided to slow down their next attempt to work for a good while. The L. & N. railroad crosses the Cumberland River at several places before coming into Harlan. It was the only line servicing the coal mines with empty coal cars and then freighting the loaded cars out. The L. & N. had built iron bridges of two and more spans across the river. Well placed charges of dynamite could paralyze the movement of trains coming into the Harlan coal fields. Dynamite was obtained and furnished to a selected group of men. To carry out this assignment they blew the center spans on two bridges. If railroad crews had honored our union by refusing to service the coal mines with empty cars, their bridges would have never been damaged. Now they would take months to repair.

The sheriff rushed to Frankfort to hold a conference with the governor to plan their strategy to halt the movements of the striking miners. He informed the governor that he had only five of his deputies left to serve the entire county and that miners were rampaging by burning and dynamiting company property and running the companies' workers out of the county. He said he had to have help before the union started murdering the miners who had returned to work. They were now barricaded in their homes, afraid to go out their door for fear of being gunned down by hidden union men. Some of them were their next door neighbors.

After the sheriff had made his plea for help, the governor ordered four companies of motorized infantry to establish martial law everywhere in Harlan County.

When our leaders learned of this, they stationed the more rugged union men at the most strategic points along the mountain roads leading into Harlan to give the infantry a welcome. Our men had been ordered not to hit any person, just to pile the bullets into the sides of the tanks and trucks to show our strength. This put fear in the teenaged boys that were to enforce martial law in our county.

The sheriff and his five deputies met the cavalcade of tanks, half tracks, and huge vans as they came rolling into the edge of town. The officer in the front vehicle came to a halt and ordered all the people off the streets. The troops riding in big G.I. trucks, with canvas tops, started piling out and came to attention at the front of each truck, waiting for their C.O. to issue them orders.

As the men stood there, two smaller vehicles with loudspeakers on top of the cabs came to a stop in front of the captains. The captain handed each driver a sheet of paper with written wording to announce to the entire county the conditions and penalties of martial law.

Two deputies were riding in each of the speaker trucks to give road directions to the many coal camps. They concealed themselves behind the drivers. With an armored escort, they started up different hollows, blasting their warnings. Troops started patrolling the streets, as troops had done the same streets before. They were in full combat uniform.

We had a large building rented from Uncle Hamp Huff to store food for the strikers. Large trucks would enter the front, a group of men would unload the food, sorting and stacking it in order. The truck would then exit in the rear. This went on every day, for some fifteen to twenty trucks would be unloaded. The patrolling troops would allow two men to the truck to make deliveries to the coal camps.

In this building Titler had set up a large meeting room for the organizers and committeemen to gather in to make plans and prepare for our next movement.

I had just got through helping load a truck with food to be sent to Molus, at the western end of the county, when two of my committeemen came in. We were to sit in on the next meeting. We loafed about the storage room until the group that had been meeting came out. My group and several other groups entered the room and took our places, waiting for Reverend Bill Clontz to open the discussion.

The meeting was getting underway and then, all at once, the door burst open and Bill Randolph, one of the sheriff's chief deputies, and four of the state military men came rushing in with drawn guns aimed at the group of us, telling us we were all under arrest for assembling without permit.

The troops searched each of us for weapons. None were found except pocket knives. They took these and started herding us through the door. There were twenty-four committeemen. Bill Clontz and George Titler and Bill Randolph were in front, leading the way. Two troopers were just through the door and moving. The other two troopers were bringing up the rear.

As I stepped through the door I fell to the left on a pile of discarded torn canvas. I rolled myself under the canvas quick and lay still. After they had gone, I came out of my hiding place and rode out of town with a food truck going to my house at Chevrolet.

My friend Jim Bodie and the other twenty-four men were locked up in the county jail. I feared for their safety. Bill Randolph had beaten two men to death in their cells and reported their deaths as due to an attempt to escape. This should be on record in the Harlan County court clerk's office.

As the people came to my home in pairs to receive their ration of food, I passed the word about what had happened in town. Some were for storming the jail and killing as many as it took to release our men. Some wanted to make bombs and slip around at night and bomb the trucks and tanks and half-tracks.

I tried to quiet the men down, telling them we had an attorney in Bell County that had connections in Washington that could get a release for the arrested men. The attorney's name was James Golden, and it was up to me to get word to him. But if I went through town I would be picked up and thrown in with them.

One of our members, a Negro, came to get his rations. I told him of James Golden and he volunteered to try to get to Pineville with a letter from me with our seal stamped on it, giving him all the details of the arrest and how I had escaped from them.

The next day all the men were released and all charges against them were dropped. My committeemen came to get their food rations and told me George Titler and Bill Clontz sent their thanks for what I had done.

I laid around home for a few days, waiting for things to quiet down about the arrest. Puttering around the house, enjoying my three children.

FOURTEEN

NO ATTEMPT had been made by any of the companies to operate their mines. The Three Point Coal Company and the Mary Helen Coal Company owned by Elmer Hall and his sister, two of the largest coal producers in Harlan, had built several long buildings near their mines to house the state guards. The bridges had been repaired and all the sidetracks were filled with empty coal cars. Work crews had repaired sections of tracks leading up the different forks from town to the many mines through the county.

Something was about to happen. Out-of-state cars were everywhere, going and coming from town with two and three people in each car. The people were strangers to this part of the country. Sometimes there would be two or three military men riding with them, or a fleet of G.I. trucks crammed with combat-dressed military men.

If one of our members was walking beside the road, the out-of-state driver would see how close he could come without hitting him, then start yelling and cussing the person. If the car happened to have military men in it, they would get out and search the person, pushing and shoving him around, with a few threats made. The person would be made to turn around and head back to where he came from. This was one of their many methods to put fear in the striking miners.

The sheriff had gathered all his deputies who had quit him earlier, and hired hundreds more. They dressed in the code of thugs—black hat, new overalls, jacket, white shirt, and under the shirt, a bullet-proof vest, blue serge pants, shiny black shoes and two big pistols. They had come back at the sheriff's promises of having the state guard to give assistance in any duty the mine owners assigned to them. Three crews to each camp and three men to a crew were to be escorted anywhere they went, with as many state guards as they wished for. All their needs would be provided for by the coal companies that were in charge of them.

A big truck loaded with union food was forced off the road by a car full of deputies. The truck went into the ditch and turned on its side. The deputies pulled the driver and his aide out and started beating them with billy sticks, causing broken ribs, arms, fingers, and big bloody bruises about the face. This started more of the deputies to doing the same things, only some of them wouldn't stop with just a beating. A lot of the truck drivers and their helpers were later found dead.

After five or six of these attacks on our food trucks, the other truckers refused to haul any more food to the camps. Within a week, miners and their families were out of food. They feared the attacks that had been made on others as they walked to town. Some of the camps were fifteen to twenty-five miles from the food that was stored in our big building. There wasn't any way to get the food to them and they had no way to come after it.

The railroad people started placing empty coal cars at all the coal mines. The work signs went up. All the cars from out of state had people that had been recruited to break the strike. The state guard had lifted some of the pressure of martial law, allowing more travel on the roads. The federal government had sent in investigators who had taken photos of a lot of things and written details of what had occurred.

Food trucks started hauling food to the hungry miners and their families again. We were getting the best of care—plenty of food, medical care, some clothing, and gas for our cars. Very few of our men returned to work when the company put up their work sign. The companies that were trying to operate with untrained crews were losing greatly.

George Titler was being approached nearly every day by the smaller operators to discuss their problems. They told him they were going broke and they wished to sign any kind of a contract, just so they could save their mines from going in bankruptcy. They were ready to discharge their deputies and break away from the state guards.

Some of the companies hated the union and would do damage to their own property and accuse the union of doing it. The company I worked for, the Blue Diamond Coal Company, caused thousands of dollars' damage to vital parts of their mines and preparation plant. The company officials would oversee the placing of dynamite and then leave a sign leading to some union man. Their insurance company would file charges against some innocent man.

I was one of the accused destroyers. I had been the underground organizer while working in their mine. From the first day I worked for them, the things I saw and heard! The way foremen drove the miners to do unnecessary work and not pay them for it. If for some reason a loader failed to load all the coal that had been cut and blasted loose in his work place, leaving it until the next day, or if it took the loader two days to load one day's quota, he would be fired or demoted to a working place with a bad overhead or water eight to ten inches deep, having to wade in it and load coal.

Some of the miners would carry their dinner pail with only water in it, leaving what little food there was to their families. I have shared my lunch many times with men that had only water for their lunch. I would tell my wife of this and she would wonder how any man could treat another man this way.

I would lay awake, too tired to get restful, and make promises to myself that if I ever got the chance, I would do all the Lord would give me power to do to avenge all the brutal treatment these poor miners were being given.

At last my chance came when Bob Hodge and Bill Clontz selected me to go underground and organize this company. The company had rehired their deputy thug, Joe Morris. He hated my guts but he feared the union until the state guards came to give him assistance in guarding the scabs and putting fear in everyone he could. The company had furnished Joe a big black Buick. His job was to drive continually back and forth, looking for some striking miner he could scare or force to go back to work.

My friend James Bodie came from town and stopped at John Keller's little store. Keller, being one of the union's strongest believers, kept us informed of all he could learn about plans and plots the thugs and military were making. Bodie had been informed by Keller that two thugs from Mary Helen Coal Company were to dynamite a drift mouth at our mine, and one of our members would be accused.

I had worked hard all day, stacking and sorting, weighing and measuring two truckloads of food. After Bodie got his food and told me this, I went to bed, tired out from all the work I'd done. Mae, having put our two older children to bed, remained up, rocking our baby to sleep. I must have fallen asleep as soon as I laid down. Mae told me later how Joe Morris and five of the state guards came bursting through the front door and four more came through the back.

Joe asked her, "Where is that God damn man of yours?"

Mae stood up, holding the baby, trying to quiet it from being scared and crying over all the noise the thugs and guards were making. They were yelling and cursing her and me, calling me a "God damn Russian Red," and a "God damn John L. Lewis bastard." She was scared and trying to tell them I was in bed asleep.

They took positions at the foot of my bed and aimed their machine guns at me, releasing the safety on them, ready to blast me through the bed. The officer of the guards was holding a sawed-off double-barrel shotgun cocked and aimed at me. Joe was shaking my feet, covering me with one of the pistols in his hand.

One of the guards, with his machine gun pointed at Mae, told her to stop the God damn baby from crying and to stay where she was at.

When I opened my eyes I thought I was dreaming. I started to rub my eyes and Joe said, "Don't you make a move, God damn you, until I tell you to."

I laid there, staring at the guards with their weapons trained on me and listening to Joe and the officer cuss at me, calling me everything they could think of. Joe felt under my pillow, searching to see if I had a gun under it. He then ordered me out of bed, telling me if I made one false move I would be blasted to hell. He had been well trained and coached on how to put people in fear and make them do what he told them to do. I was doing just exactly as he told me.

Joe reached for my overalls and searched each pocket, finding only a sack of smoking tobacco and a small pocket knife. He threw these on the floor and handed me my overalls and shirt and said, "Put them on, you damn bastard." I nervously put them on and stepped in my boots. I hadn't said a word, just doing as I was told, fearing for the safety of my wife and babies.

Joe and the officer, taking hold of each arm, steered me through the house, with two guards leading, holding their machine guns ready to blast their way through any opposition. The other two were coming behind me with their weapons aimed at my back.

The house was high off the ground and as we came down the steps several guards came from under it, carrying their rifles on the ready.

They shoved me in the back seat of Joe's Buick and a guard sat on each side of me. Joe drove while the officer told me I wouldn't be so God damn much trouble to them when they got through with me. I never asked where they were taking me. Sitting there between the two guards I feared they might start beating me.

The Buick pulled up near the main bookkeeper's office and they herded me in, shoving and pushing me. When I was shoved through the door, I fell. Joe started to kick me, but the higher officer (I think he was a captain) held him back.

They made me sit, and the superintendent for the mine handed me a sheet of blank paper and a pencil and told me to print my name at the bottom of it. He then handed me another sheet with a hand-printed message on it. He told me to read it good and then print it on the other page, word for word. I looked at it. My name was at the bottom. It looked like the way I print, but I hadn't printed it. I shook my head and asked, "What in the hell are you trying to do to me? I never wrote this note. If you intend to take me over the mountain, you might as well get started, for I'm not going to print this note and I'm sure as hell not going to sign my name to any damn thing."

I raised up and was pushed back down by the officer that had brought me in. He was toying with a long piece of leaded rubber hose, telling me that if I refused to do what I had been told he would take me out and beat the hell out of me.

Each man in there was cussing me except the captain. I knew they meant for me to deny the note and try to make alibis or to escape so they could have an excuse to beat me or take me over the mountain and kill me. This had happened to a lot of striking miners who had given resistance to the thugs and the guards.

The guard with the hose said, "Let me work him over and he'll be damn glad to own up to printing that note." He kept slapping the hose in his hand and every now and then hitting the table with it, looking down at me and calling me a "God damn Russian redneck" and a "union bastard." I was expecting him to hit me anytime. I told him he was nothing but a damn thug wearing a guard uniform. He then grabbed me by the nape of the neck and raised his arm to bring the leaded hose down on me.

The captain grabbed his arm and called him a damn fool. "You know you can't do this with all these people around. Take him back home and wait for another chance." He knew that people up and down the street had seen them enter my house and force me to go with them. They feared some of our people the same as we feared them.

They started me to the door and Joe Morris got hold of my arm and said, "I'll take him back."

I locked my arms around a large pipe and refused to ride with him. Joe tugged on my arm, trying to tear me loose. The captain ordered two guards to ride back up the hollow to protect me.

I thought I had gotten the worst cussing that ever was, until Joe started in on me as he drove me back home. The other dressed-up thugs couldn't come up with the things Joe called me. I expected any minute for him to stop and drag me out and do whatever he wanted to do to me. The two guards in the back seat never said a word all the way back up the hollow.

Mae was still up, with the house all lit up, afraid to stay there in the dark after what had happened earlier. One of the guards walked me to the gate and I dashed in the house and turned all the lights off. I wasn't wanting to give them a lit-up target if they wanted to fire at me and say it must have been a ricochet bullet that hit me.

Mae had kept the children asleep and was pacing the floor, wondering if I would be back or not. We sat in the front room with the lights out, trying to settle the nervousness that had built up in us, when we heard a lot of commotion across the street. A post light had the street lit up good, and by peeking through the window we could see what was going on.

The same guards that had raided my house and taken me were forcing my neighbor, Tip Allen, into Joe Morris's car. He wasn't going willingly. One was forcing his head in and Joe was pushing on his rear. His wife and his older children were crying and begging for them not to beat him or hurt him.

I couldn't go to his aid. If I had gone out my gate they would have shot me down. All I could do was watch what they were doing and report it to George Titler or Bob Hodge. Later I found out they tried to force Tip to sign a statement that he saw me print that note.

The next morning, after the guards had made their round up the hollow, me and Earl Thompson, one of my committeemen, sneaked past the bathhouse and headed for the mountain. Crossing it where we came to the edge of the river, we were now near the town. We separated, Earl walking the road to town and me wading the edge of the river, ducking down and hiding every time a car passed. This way we reached the back of our headquarters building.

I pounded on the door until someone opened it. I told the man we had to see George Titler or Bob Hodge and I didn't want to be seen in town. Earl and I stayed where we were until Titler and Hodge came. I went over everything with them.

Bob and Bill Clontz had taken pictures of several victims, some dead and others beaten till their face looked like a bloody mass of meat, some with broken arms and fingers. They wanted Tip Allen and me to sign a complaint, and with all this Bill Clontz was to go to Washington and present it to the congressman from our district.

Bob suggested we go to Sally Malicott's restaurant for dinner. Earl went to the front to check the streets for patrolling guards. We didn't want to be stopped by them and questioned. Only two people were allowed to be together on the streets. The guards would stop them and question and search them if they looked like they were not merchants or regular town people.

It was about three blocks to Sally's restaurant. I left first, wearing a white butcher apron someone had left near a large stack of salt pork. Whoever had left it there had borrowed it from Dave Middleton's meat store next door. It had a "Middleton's Fresh Meats" sign across the top of it in red thread. Titler and Bob got a laugh when I tied it around my waist and started down the street.

I passed two or three pairs of guards on my way. They were walking slowly, eyeing everything that moved. They just glanced at me and saw the lettering on the apron and nodded a greeting as I passed them. The others followed. Titler and Earl walked together, then Bob and Bill Clontz came.

Several guards were in the restaurant having lunch. I motioned to Sally with a nod of my head that I wanted to use the private room. She understood quick what I meant. She went to the kitchen and unlocked the door that allowed entrance to the bathroom from the kitchen.

The others came on through the bathroom, and Sally took our orders. Earl and I were hungry from the hiking from Chevrolet across the mountain, and the walk along the river bank had took all the pep from us.

Titler got to explaining what our next plans were to be. He wanted everything set up at each camp, with all the committeemen knowing their assignments. While Bill Clontz was to be gone to Washington, he wanted me to go back home and in any way I could avoid being questioned by thugs and guards. I was just to stay at home. He would stay in contact with me through the food truck driver. He said, "I have been kept informed about the delegates from the coal companies trying to influence Washington bigwigs with bribes and lies concerning Harlan County."

But with the photos and data Bill was taking, things were sure to happen. He had photos of over a hundred different men going in and out of the military headquarters. They were taken with a long-range camera. These men would go in wearing just ordinary clothes and come out dressed in a captain's or lieutenant's uniform and then be driven to some coal company and report to the mine management for orders.

We had a few underground men that had worked themselves into some of the companies' confidence who would be trusted with evidence and records of all the killings, beatings, and the dynamiting of their own property by these professional men wearing captain's uniforms. This information Titler had gotten from our agents who were working as bookkeepers, mine foremen, and store managers. He had a way of reaching them that was unknown to any of the miners. Only a few of his most trusted organizers were allowed to know of it.

Bill Clontz and Bob Hodge had to be taken to Pineville city hospital for treatment of a very dangerous disease that was spreading throughout the county. The commanding officer of the state military guards was asked to allow a military ambulance to take them at once to avoid spreading the disease. The officer dispatched an ambulance and an escort to rush the two victims to Pineville for treatment. Bob and Bill entered the front door of the hospital and went on through the back to a waiting car with a United States marshal in it. They had a small suitcase each, filled with clothes and with documents of all the material Titler had gathered concerning the things the coal companies had directed the thugs and state military to do to the people of Harlan County.

When they arrived in Washington, the marshal steered them to different congressmen and a meeting was called. John L. Lewis, the president of the United Mine Workers' Union, was present with a lot more information. With all this proof, with sworn affidavits, along with most of Harlan County's elected officials, indictments were made against most of the coal operators, to be tried in a federal court in London, Kentucky. The officials were big landowners and mineral owners, leasing their properties to coal operators and collecting huge sums of money in return for the privilege of operating their mines any way they wanted to.

The thugs were known by name. The disguised state military officers were brought before the court to give testimony of the orders given to them by the sheriff and the operators.

The sheriff, during his campaign, had worked both sides. He had promised the operators full protection against the union for their support in the election. He had also promised the union that no thugs would be allowed in Harlan County. He said, "Each and every person will have the protection of my office when I'm elected." He said there would be no more of the false arrests and beatings like those the previous sheriff had allowed to be done.

He won the election by a great margin, but he wasn't in office two weeks when he started rehiring all the thugs that had worked under the old sheriff, giving them orders to do anything the operators requested.

The operators started issuing orders for certain members of the union to be taken out of the county, or to fire into their homes and scare them into leaving. The sheriff had a crew of them to dynamite Bill Clontz's home. Bill was away when it happened and no one was hurt.

The only promise the sheriff kept was to the operators. A lot of our union men were sent to prison for crimes the thugs had done. The county judge, Morris Saylor, was one of the wealthiest coal and land owners in Harlan County. When a union man was brought before him he was automatically found guilty of any charge the thugs filed against him.

With the evidence our union men furnished, a lot of operators got suspended sentences and a few thugs got short prison terms. Some of our convicted union men were released. It was a great victory for our union. The governor withdrew all the state guards. The thugs that weren't given prison terms left Harlan County. Some of the thugs that left soon met a torturing death by unknown persons. One of them was Joe Morris, the thug at Chevrolet, where I worked.

It wasn't long until all the operators were begging for the union to meet with them. A contract was made and all the coal companies signed it. The mines began working under their new contract, eager to treat their employees with respect. The foremen that had driven the miners before with threats of the thugs would now ask them nicely to perform the different kinds of work it took to produce coal.

Living conditions improved with the raise we got in pay, and the whole county started to prosper.

The sheriff met death in a city somewhere in Kentucky. The cause of his death was never determined. Some people thought he might have tortured himself to death. When the news of his death reached Harlan, all the local unions called their members from the mines to meet in Harlan for an all-day celebration. Rejoicing were groups of miners that still wore scars or had to walk with the aid of crutches or canes, and widows with their broods of small children that had lost their husbands to the death-dealing thugs that took their orders from the sheriff.

Soon after this celebration I was offered a better job across the mountain in Letcher County, where my wife was raised. I accepted it and moved to a coal camp at Carbon Glow, Kentucky. I worked in the mines eight hours a day and operated a company barbershop at night. Carbon Glow being a long way from the nearest town or village, I thought the barbershop pay would be a boost to my earnings. But eventually the people there didn't like my style of barbering, or didn't like me, and I soon moved back to Harlan.

I went to work at Molus, loading coal. The seam of coal I was working in averaged thirty-four inches thick. It was very difficult for me to hunker down on my knees and perform the task of shoveling coal into mining cars thirty inches high.

The mine superintendent, checking on my daily production and my regular way of reporting for work, called me into his office to offer me a better-paying job. The demand for coal was increasing every day and he wanted me to develop more working places by using a crew of men on a second shift. The pay increase would be according to the tonnage. The second shift would load and then prepare the working places for the next shift.

I was earning more money working at night and could afford a better place to live. But Mae and the children being alone at night, I feared for their safety and comfort. I located a big comfortable house about three miles further away. I knew I would have to walk to and from my job, but I was satisfied with the comfort and safety my family had.

Mae and I started storing food again. We canned every vegetable and fruit we raised on the small farm we were renting. I had ordered five hundred baby chicks. We had a huge barn to house them in. It wasn't long before we had a fresh milk cow and some nice fat hogs for butchering. Working at nights and helping her with all this preparing of food during the day gave me the satisfaction of security in the future if the coal mines slacked down on work.

During the day, when not sleeping, I was working around the house. Our two boys and our daughter enjoyed themselves tending the hogs, petting the young calf, and hunting hens' nests in the barn loft. Some days they would find an old hen setting on her eggs and they would try to get the eggs from under her. The old hen would flog them and they would come running to the house telling us the old mommy hen was having babies. Sometimes an egg would be burst with a newly hatched chick lying in it.

Things like this made life worth living. Mae and I were having the best years of our lives through these times, enjoying our children and not being obligated to anyone but ourselves.

Our fourth child, Benjamin, was born here. He was just like the others, perfect in form and healthy. While Mae was recovering from the childbirth one of her sisters came to help care for her and the children. She took over the management of the house and she soon had all of us depending on her for everything we needed. She cared for Mae like she was the baby instead of little Benjamin. The other children loved her and would help do the cleaning and outside chores.

After Mae gained her strength we began planning what to plant in the vegetable garden. We let the children make suggestions. Bill, the oldest, wanted to plant anything that didn't need much hoeing or help to grow. He said, "It keeps me busy taking care of all the other things." I was teaching him and the others how to make do with what you had to do with. We shared our chores and everyone was happy doing their part.

During the late summer the mines started slowing down to one and two days a week. All the coal buyers had bought enough coal to stock their supply yards for the next two years. They were in a position now to bargain with the operators for a lower price for coal. The coal market was closing down. The operators tried to make coal sales overseas and offered to stockpile coal for northern cities and big utilities on credit. When this failed, the operators stockpiled coal by the thousands of tons, using up all their profits from the past till they had to shut their mines down.

The miners living in camps were soon without money and food. They depended for their day-by-day existence on their daily earnings, not planning ahead for a slowup in mining. Government relief

140

programs were set up in most of the county. The coal companies would advance each miner one dollar a day so as to help tide them over until the coal market opened up, not wanting them to leave and seek work somewhere else.

The little farm I lived on was about four miles from the company's camp, and I seldom made trips there. When I did have to go it was to get news of the working situation and maybe a bag of candy or fresh fruit for my young farmers, the children. They sure were learning to take hold of things to do on the little farm. I guess I must have been the proudest person alive with my close family around me.

Some of my close friends back in the organization days came to see me, George Gilbert and Reverend Bill Clontz. They had a message from George Titler, wanting me to hire in for work at Benham, Kentucky, and secretly select miners to break away from the company's union and sign an agreement with United Mine Workers' Union.

Benham mines were owned by International Harvester Company, which used their own coal at their steel mills and factories. Their coal mine had to operate every day to supply them.

The hiring agent at Benham was to check the background of any applicant wishing to work there. Clontz and Gilbert had done a good job of getting my history with the union done away with. My application was accepted and I was put to work as a track man, keeping mining rail track repaired and underground roofs supported with steel beams and huge round posts at each end holding loose slate and rock from falling on the tracks underneath.

I was given a crew of six men for this work. Some of them soon began to trust my leadership. News of their willingness to work as I suggested reached the head mine foreman. He heard how I was getting along with my crew and about the safety precautions I was taking. We were doing everything possible to keep the haulways clear for the production of coal.

The head mine foreman met each Monday morning with all the production foremen to discuss working programs and ways to make each employee safe while working underground. Me being in charge of a crew, I was asked to attend these meetings. I would sit in the back at these meetings and listen to all the suggestions on increasing the tonnage per unit and about safety programs to insure each miner enough first aid training to assist a fellow miner with any kind of injury until professional aid could arrive. The chairman of these meetings would ask for ideas on all these suggestions to be made by any of the men present. Sometimes he would point out a certain foreman to give his idea on how to perform a program and keep the miners happy.

I was called on to explain the system I was using with the crew under me. I explained I was just using good horse sense, treating each man with having enough knowledge to understand the dangers of the different assignments and how important it was to do a good job. I would listen to any of their ideas on dangerous roof repairing, and soon learned I was getting better work done. The men talked safety to each other as they worked.

I hadn't moved to Benham yet, and Reverend Clontz kept in contact with me on the progress I was making on my new assignment for the union. He had informers in the Benham office that would keep him posted on all the company union's actions.

I was soon appointed over all the mine's track and the timbering crews that kept the roof safe from faulty overhead rock slate. Taking on this more important work was demanding more time. Some days would require twelve hours' work. The superintendent asked me to move into Benham so I would be nearer in case of an emergency.

Clontz and Gilbert were doing a good job of keeping my union activities quiet. I soon began feeling the men out about the difference between the company union and the United Mine Workers' Union. Nearly everyone I talked to wanted the United Mine Workers' Union because it was more demanding on the owners of the mines and the pay was a few dollars more on the day. They would say they were ready any time to take a vote to change the unions. I started slipping these decided men membership cards in the United Mine Workers' Union.

The superintendent got news of what I had been doing and called me into his office to explain my actions against the other union. I told him I had over half the employees signed up with United Mine Workers' Union, and a federal court order demanding an election to decide which union would be in power, which also stated that no action would be taken against the men that wanted to change unions.

I had 326 miners signed up. The company employed 574. I presented the superintendent with a copy of the contract he was to sign if we won the election. He commended me on the way I had infiltrated into company trust and become so powerful with the employees.

The election was held and we lost due to a lot of promises being made to men with long-standing service to the company, such as a lower age limit on retirement and a company house to live in when they retired.

The job I had been doing was terminated and I was offered another job at the same rate of pay in a new section of the mine. The superintendent didn't hold a grudge against me. He liked the way I got work performed in a safe manner and wanted me to stay with the company. He said, "I'd rather have you working for me so I can keep tabs on my future!"

I began to understand his position with the company. He was put in charge of the mines because he was the best coal producer the company could find. He knew very little about the moods and actions of the miners. He only met them when one of his inside foremen brought one to his office for commendations or promotion.

FIFTEEN

ON DECEMBER 7, 1941, Japan bombed Pearl Harbor. All the young men were called to the different branches of the armed forces, leaving the older men to do the mining. There was a great demand for coal and the producing mines weren't meeting the demand. Thousands of small truck mines started opening up all over the coal fields, trucking their coal to the railheads for shipment to the eager steel mills and factories.

Nearly everything you had to have was rationed by the government. Workers at most places were frozen to their jobs, if the companies they were working for requested it. I had been asked earlier by my superintendent to attend a mine foremen's school at nearby Lynch, and I was awarded with a mine foreman's certificate, giving me legal right to govern the work of any coal mine. This has always been the top ambition of all young miners.

The superintendent put me in charge of production on the night shift, working the same places the day shift worked, using the same number of workers the day foreman used. I don't like to hear anyone boast of himself and I don't intend to brag on myself, but all the production foremen with the superintendents included gave me a big party for the effort I was doing to increase tonnage and for having no injuries to any of the workers under my supervision.

And then it happened. I was riding from the face of a coal loader's place of work, hunkered down on my knees on the riding stirrup of a low-vein locomotive. A short piece of steel rail was lying alongside of the track. It caught my pants leg and tore on down, crushing my boot and nearly tearing my left foot off at the ankle.

The company's head doctor wanted to take the foot off. His assistant disagreed. He went to work cleaning and placing the tendons together, removing chips of bone, wiring the bigger bones, and replacing the heel string with some kind of fiber that would allow flesh to adhere to it!

I had a hard time explaining the accident to the other foremen and the safety committee—me being the first to get hurt after having the best safety record of all the foremen.

I was laid up in the hospital about six weeks. Before being released, my doctor handed me a pair of crutches and taught me how to use them. I hobbled around on these crutches for about two weeks, then the doctor fitted a steel brace around my ankle that would allow me to stand on it. I traded him the crutches for a good strong cane. Here I'd go, slinging that club foot and wobbling on my cane. I soon got my strength back, but was not able to go back to work. I got about half of what I had earned when working, so my family was about to come up short on a few things we needed.

A lot of miners would plant big gardens up in the mountains, using a hoe to dig the soil loose. This kind of planting was slow and hard work, but they managed to raise a lot of vegetables, and corn to fatten a few hogs. I began thinking I could help ease their work and let them raise a lot more with less effort if they had a small mule to do the plowing and to sled the things they had grown off the mountains.

It was forty miles from Benham to Isom, Kentucky. Isom boasted of the lowest priced farm mules and the best ones in the state. I told some of the coal mining farmers I was going to ride a bus over the mountain and bring back a string of mules to sell to the men who were farming up in the mountains. Each man I talked to wanted me to bring him the smallest mule I could get. I contracted with four men for the sale of four small mules, buying them at a bargain price and being allowed to make a profit of $10 a head.

I got to the stock pens early, waddling along, slinging my club foot and putting more weight on my cane than was necessary. I went from one stall of mules to another, just eyeing each mule and waiting for the auctioneer to start the bidding. I guess it was me being lame and the big club foot that caused the other bidders to not bid against me. I bought five small mules dirt cheap and a fairly new saddle for nearly nothing.

I had to cross two small mountains and big Pine Mountain to reach Benham. I strung the four mules together behind me and started for Benham. I was pushing along at a fast gait, not wanting to stay overnight along the road. The first fifteen miles put me about half-way up Pine Mountain, where an old mountain farmer tended big hillsides of corn. I rode into his barn lot and offered to buy some grain for the mules and some food for myself.

The old man, Jim Trent, refused to take my money, but he fed and pumped water for the mules, and Mrs. Trent fixed me a good dinner. I tried to get them to take pay. I told them I would be stopping again. Just as soon as I delivered this string, I'd be going back for more mules and maybe a cow or two. Mr. Trent said he would charge a little for the next trip but this one was free. I thanked them both, saddled a different mule, and rode on to Benham.

As I rode along with the mule train strung out on the side of the road, avoiding the heaviest traffic because the mules were a bit skittish and afraid of cars, I was getting eager to get out of the saddle. My tail felt like a swarm of bees had settled on it and each one had left its stinger stuck in it.

The next evening the men came to take charge of their mules. Each man was pleased with what I had chosen him, including the low price I had paid. They gladly paid me my $10 profit for each mule.

Making this kind of money made me feel like a big livestock dealer, but my butt was still sore. My mule buyers got a big laugh as they watched me try to sit down on my hip instead of my sore scalded tail. I felt like all the skin had been rubbed off and red pepper had been rubbed in to heal it.

I turned the fifth mule loose in a big pasture on the side of a steep hill. Him being the only animal there, he started roaming all over the fenced-in land. After following the fence line completely, he stopped beneath a large tree. Standing in a level worn path, just above the fence, he started stomping at flies. His shod hoof coming down on an exposed root caused him to slide from the path. His head went between two large bushes and his hind parts rolled against the wire fence. The bushes being strong enough to hold him when his body hit the fence, it broke his neck. I was the loser of a good mule.

This took nearly all my profit from my first venture as a big livestock dealer. Here I was, nearly broke, with a dead mule on hand, a club foot, not well enough to go back to work, and a sore rump.

About all the coal miners in Benham were allowed to keep a milk cow and hogs. The cows mostly were all pastured together on a big cleared mountain with plenty of streams through it and a big shed to house them in at milking time. Each evening the miners that owned cows would gather at the milking shed to swap tales and trade knives.

I hobbled up to where a group was sitting, chewing their tobacco and whittling with razor keen knives, waiting for their cows to come out of the hills to be milked. Their tales got started on raising hogs and the many different breeds that could be fattened the cheapest. The Spotted Pole was agreed to be the fastest growing and the easiest to fatten. Some of the men were wishing they had one or two for butchering. I told them I could get any number they wanted at a cheap price per head, but I wanted to make a little money doing it. They agreed to let me make $8 on each hog I brought them.

I went to the credit union and discussed the financing with Bob Hern, the manager, about borrowing $200 and the use of his truck to haul them in. I got the money and the truck. He also wanted me to bring him a big sow with a litter of pigs. His truck was small and I rigged a second deck to it so I could bring back a double load.

I arrived at Isom stockyards early and started pen hooking. That's buying from the truckers before they unload their stock in the sale pen, knocking the auctioneer out of his selling fee. I loaded both decks with pigs and shoats of different breeds. I got Bob Hern a big Poland China sow with ten sucking pigs, and headed back to Benham. I parked the truck in front of the credit union's building to show the hogs to miners as they came from work. I hadn't bought the size the other miners wanted and all of these were for sale. I sold the entire load in less than an hour for a profit of over a hundred dollars.

The following week I got Bob's truck and went back to the Isom stockyards. As before, I pen hooked another load. This time I got the size and breed the other men wanted and had three left for myself. Everybody I had sold to was pleased with the price they paid and didn't mind paying me the agreed fee for my work getting them.

My foot was healed enough for me to wear a shoe and I was eager to go back to the mines. The doctor examined my foot and gave me a back-to-work slip, requesting I be put on light duty with very little walking.

The section I had been running had a gathering place for small pumps to discharge in and two big powerful pumps to pick up the water and pump it to the outside of the mine. Someone had to stay with these two pumps to keep them greased and oiled and then just sit and listen to them hum and grind. The hardest thing I had to do was stay awake. I stayed on this pump job until my foot was completely healed and I was ready to take over my regular job. The

147

superintendent insisted I stay off it for at least another month. Our fourth son, Dave, was born about this time.

The war was getting worse. The Japanese had captured the Philippines and several young men from Benham had been taken prisoner. Any paper you looked at was covered with news of the fronts where our men were fighting. Every young man that could manage to get deferred was doing it. Some faked an illness, others used their religion. Some would commit crimes so they would be sent to prison to keep from being drafted.

The way the war was going, I figured it might take another Jones or two to win the war. My old friend Reverend Bill Clontz was chairman of the draft registration. After a few sleepless nights I decided to call Clontz and have him call me for volunteer service to the armed forces. Some say that the atomic bomb caused the Japanese to surrender, but I think they heard that the Joneses were coming and gave up.

I left for naval training the next week. On my way by train to the Great Lakes naval training center, the engine hit a tractor trailer loaded with bathroom fixtures. A fireman was killed and fifty or more passengers were injured. The entire train of coaches was wrecked. The one I was riding in was off the rails and bumping along on the ties. This happened in Dyer, Indiana. The naval center sent a convoy of trucks to pick up their recruits, about 300 of us.

It was after midnight when we arrived at Great Lakes. We were herded to big barracks buildings, dog tired and hungry. There wasn't anything in the buildings but a long table and a bench on each side. About sixty men were assigned to each building. There was nowhere to sit or lay down. We hadn't eaten since breakfast and had had nothing to drink all day.

The men were on edge and wishing they were back in the coal mines, letting someone else fight the war. As we were standing there, waiting for orders to get our sleeping gear and something to eat, a petty officer came in, hopped on the table, and began strutting back and forth and calling us a bunch of damn dumb hillbillies and a lot more fighting words. He was laying out the rules of navy training, the do's and don'ts. The first one was no smoking unless he said we could.

The petty officer ordered each one of us to line up at one end of the barracks and place a roll of steel wool under one foot and start rubbing it back and forth on the floor, making the wood shiny and new looking. He had us do this for over an hour, then he ordered us to bathe without soap or towels.

I've never understood why the government, which we were willing to fight and die for, could knowingly let someone harass a group of people like we were being done. Some of the boys that had never missed a meal or done without sleep began to tire out. The petty officer would order them to continue doing whatever they had been told to do or he would have them locked in the brig.

We managed to stay on our feet the rest of the night. A whistle sounded for breakfast and we lined up at a big mess hall and were handed a tin plate and a mess kit cup, then passed through a chow line that served whole boiled potatoes and white boiled navy beans, with a thick slice of bread and a mess kit cup of black cold coffee. It was hard to get down, but we were so weak from loss of sleep and food that anything we could get in our stomachs felt good.

The rest of the day we were herded through long lines of doctors as if we were animals, being examined for everything and given shots that caused some to pass out. I began to think that if it took this kind of treatment to get to fight in the war, I was ready for Hitler and the other enemies to take over whatever they wanted.

I could go on describing this boot camp treatment for several pages and not get half of it explained, so I'll go from here to my first ship, the S.S. Arizona, a merchant ship. I was a gunner in the U.S. Navy armed guard aboard this merchant ship. My first trip to sea was an experience I'll never forget. There must have been a thousand ships in the convoy I was in, made up of all our allied nations. The outer columns were mostly heavily armed light cruisers, giving the convoy long-range protection.

We had been at sea six days when we came within a mine field. Several ships were damaged before the mine sweepers came in and cleared the lanes.

Sometime during the night our ship started rolling and pitching. It would shake like it was falling apart when the big propeller would raise out of the water. The alert buzzer sounded and all hands reported to G.Q. (general quarters).

The seas were rough, the ship would take a nosedive when riding a large wave, and then, rolling from side to side, would head straight up another large swell. All the hatches were closed but a lot of water was in the passages. No lamps were on and you had to feel your way from place to place. Some of the first-timers at sea kept yelling we were sinking. You could hear the great waves splash against the bulkhead with giant force.

After hours of being tossed about, it began to calm. The lamps were lit and the ship was riding the swells more smoothly. All hands were called on deck and each crew was given a special assignment to check the security of the cargo that was lashed on deck. Some of the lines had snapped and a few lashing rings had been torn from the deck, leaving big gaping holes, allowing water to pour through to decks below.

The gun crews started cleaning the torn and shredded canvas that had been used to protect our guns. We opened the breeches of each gun and with oiled reamers we cleared the barrels of all the moisture that had been blown into them. All the ammo was checked and found to be unmoved by the rolling of the ship.

The cooks were having a job cleaning up the galley and getting breakfast started. It didn't take them long to have plenty of coffee ready. It seemed like the old salts could live on coffee and strong pipe tobacco.

The swells had smoothed and the ship was knifing through the calm sea with the grace of a great swan. All cargo was made fast and the guns taken care of. Crew after crew would have breakfast. While eating, there was much talk about the storm. The older men who had been at sea many years would tell of storms that would make the one we had just had seem like an April shower.

On these merchant ships the navy gun crew were treated equally with the merchantmen on board. Our meals were chosen from a big menu of many different foods that could be prepared any way you liked. A mess boy would take your order and serve you, just like you were in some big fine restaurant.

The rest of this voyage was smooth sailing. The ocean on a windless morning, with the sun gleaming on it, would look like a great sheet of glass. Every now and then, a school of porpoises would appear alongside of the ship. Gulls started circling the ship, splattering the deck (or anything else that was beneath them) with their droppings.

As we cruised to Land's End, England, U.S. fighter planes gave aerial support to the ships, circling and dipping their wings in friendly greetings. The ships that were laden with war supplies anchored offshore, waiting for formation orders from our rear admiral to cross the English Channel to Cherbourg, France.

The scuttlebutt was that we had to stay anchored for five days where we were and then rendezvous with other ships for the crossing. The merchantmen were allowed to have liberty while we were anchored, but the navy men on board had to stay with our guns. One or two navy boys dressed in merchant marine uniforms and slipped ashore, bringing back a few bottles of spirits tucked in their socks, their bell-bottom trousers covering them.

During my off-duty hours while we were anchored, I began writing letters to my wife and children, trying to let them know where I was and where we were headed for. Mae and I had worked out a code that only she and myself could understand. All our mail was censored but I was never questioned on any letter I wrote. Mae was kept informed of all my voyages and most of the actions I was engaged in.

About midnight on our fifth day of this wait, the alert buzzer sounded and all hands gathered for a briefing of our duties and the dangers of attacks by U-boats, aerial strafing, and floating mines. The anchor was raised and the ship started easing out. There were over 200 ships anchored here; all had running lights fore and aft.

The other ships we were to rendezvous with had been hidden in an inland cove. The point we sailed from was supposed to be directly across the channel from Cherbourg. The U.S. Navy had hundreds of craft there—destroyers, battleships, light cruisers, sea-tugs—every kind of vessel the navy had was there for the invasion.

All the navy ships raised anchor and moved out, the merchant ships following in a V formation, with mine sweepers skimming the water. All guns were manned and everything was on the ready for surface or aerial attack.

Dark clouds made the skies black and no lights were seen on any of the ships. Every now and then you could spot a ship when the fog would lift a little. The only way you could know it was a ship was from the wake it left, of foaming, phosphorous water. When you could get a glimpse of one, it looked like a ghost ship.

The column of ships we were in had been moving about two hours when very faint explosions were heard. Shortly they grew louder and nearer. A grayness started lighting the skies and the nearest columns of ships could be seen. The continuous roar coming from the big battleships was beginning to increase, and pink flashes could be seen in the grayness of the sky.

Mine sweepers were destroying floating mines, causing great waves to come rolling in every direction. The merchant ships were ordered to turn back to England and stay in port and wait for further orders. The destroyers and big battleships kept pounding the shores of France, driving the Germans inland, and the L.S.T.s started beaching. With aerial support, our big tanks began knocking out the enemy's strongholds. The marines moving in in the rear were destroying all other objects the fleeing Germans had left behind.

The invasion was a success, the channel had been cleared of U-boats and floating mines, and the merchant ships were ordered to continue their crossing to France. When we got in sight of the shores, the anchors were dropped and the heavier pieces of cargo were transferred to smaller craft. The foods and other lighter cargo in the holds were loaded into ducks. A duck is a floating jeep with powerful telescopes.

The wreckage of all the docks within view was burning, and floating bodies of the enemy could be seen. Small boats went about, picking them from the water. Search-and-destroy troops were moving inland, with all modes of land fighting equipment, chasing the Germans and blowing up ammunition in underground storage.

Fighter planes kept coming in irregular formation, strafing and sometimes dropping bombs on large installation lots and hurriedly built barracks. It looked like the whole city of Cherbourg and the surrounding country were being leveled off and burned.

It took several days to empty the ships and clean the holds. While the merchantmen did this, the gun crews cleaned their guns, chipping the paint down to bare metal, then applying a new coat of battleship gray. All the electrical firing wires were checked and all the ammunition was checked and repacked.

The fires on shore that had been burning with such force were now just small wisps of smoke. The armored division had driven the enemy far back into the mountains. The clean-up units were taking a few prisoners and capturing machine gun bunkers.

Liberty launches were taking sailors ashore for twelve-hour liberty. I went the second day to view the city's demolished ports and buildings. If you've never seen a war-torn city it would be hard for me to describe the destruction that can be caused by the bombing and shelling from the air and sea. I walked as far as I could out on a bombed dock, and could see countless bodies, bloated and bobbing in the water. Small craft were working through the wreckage recovering them. Many thousands of the enemy were killed, along with a lot of the French people that were being forced to work at the docks. Several enemy ships had been sunk and some were yet burning from within.

On our way back to England, the masts of many ships could be seen that had been sunk by U-boats and floating mines. Some of them were American vessels that could be identified by the assembly of the liners. Our ship docked in Wales and we took on fuel and food supplies. Big pumps furnished fresh water for ballast to keep the ship from riding high and to give it buoyancy.

The voyage back to the States was calm, with only a few hard rains, and it was cold. The convoy started separating about three days from New York. Our ship, the *S.S. Arizona*, tied up in Brooklyn dry docks for a major overhaul. Half the gun crew were allowed leaves. Me being one of the lucky ones, I got a ten-day leave home.

I was anxious to see my family. After all the hugging and kissing, Mae and the children all wanted me to tell of my trip overseas. I didn't want to tell them of all the hard training I had had to go through and the many times I had wished I was back working in the coal mines or buying livestock and reselling it. I just told them of the different things I had seen and how nice it was aboard ship, and the size of the convoys. I was busy till midnight answering a thousand questions. Dave was the baby, but the others wouldn't let me hold him; they were climbing all over me and I loved it.

SIXTEEN

I ENJOYED MY LEAVE and reported back to the ship so the others could have their leave. The ship had been raised and a steep gangplank had been put in. It was raised so high it was hard to recognize it as the ship I had sailed on. Shipbuilders were replating the decks that had been damaged during the storms at sea, and loose rivets were removed all over the ship. The rat-a-tat-tat of the riveters could be heard all over the ship like machine gun fire. The galley was being redone, with all new stoves, pots, and pans—everything the cook needed to use in his kitchen was being installed. All the ship's personnel had to eat off the ship at nearby restaurants while the galley was being rebuilt. New quarters were being put in for the gun crew, with double bunks. All the hammocks were taken out and a big shiny smoking table was put in the center of each crew's quarters.

The ship was completely repaired and inspected by its owners and was soon loaded with all sorts of foods—thousands of cases of boneless chicken, beef, pork, juices, and hundreds of other good foods. The decks were stashed with small steam locomotives.

The convoy was formed. Three days out at sea, word got around that we were going to Holland and Belgium. This convoy was much larger than the other one. It was smooth sailing for about a week. The sea had been just like a velvet field, with small riffles waving beneath the surface. The wind was calm and warm. An old salt, the ship's carpenter, said this was the calmness before the storm. He looked to the northern skies and said, "We'll come into a storm around midnight. With a lot of snow." I could never understand what he saw in the northern skies. But he sure hit it on the head.

When I was called to go on midnight sea watch, the coxswain told me to wear foul-weather gear with a poncho. I climbed the ladders to the main deck, going to our mess quarters for a cup of coffee before going on watch. The relief watchmen came in, shaking snow and ice from their clothes and blowing on their hands. They told the coxswain nothing could be seen, the snow was falling so fast you couldn't see two feet in front of you. The coxswain checked with the bridge and was told to keep all naval personnel off the open decks until the storm had passed. My next watch was six hours off and I crawled back into my bunk.

At breakfast all the talk was about the quick change in the weather. I had seen sudden storms back on the mountain, but I'd never seen it change from summer to winter overnight.

After it became daylight the snow stopped and all hands began to clear the deck. Places facing the storm had snow piled up four and five foot thick. Pumps were started and heavy hose soon had the deck and all the deck cargo clear. The sun was promising another warm day.

The convoy started separating, going to different ports. About twenty-five ships with ours pointed our way to Antwerp. Buzz bombs and rockets were being launched from somewhere in Holland. Antiaircraft would fire on them, using tracer bullets to explode them in the air. The buzz bombs were exploding all around. Some were aimed at Scotland and England. I saw some craters where they had exploded and you could have put a battleship in the hole.

The waterways in Holland and Belgium were very narrow for the big ships to pass through. The Dutch people lined the edges, wanting the Americans to toss them anything for exchange for a pair of Dutch wooden shoes. I thought it very odd the people all wore wooden shoes. I tossed enough bars of soap to receive six pairs. My wife has some of them yet.

Army people took over unloading the ship. A big net would be lowered into the hold by a power winch. The net would be piled full of cases and bundles of cargo to be raised and swung out onto a big two-wheel cart drawn by the biggest horses I had ever seen. Some looked to weigh over a ton. The drivers used only one check-rein. The loads they moved would weigh three to five tons. The big horses, with little effort, could move the load easily to waiting trucks and railroad cars.

Pleasures were hard to come by in Antwerp. Our officer allowed liberty for half the gun crew every twenty-four hours. We were instructed to obey all civil and military laws and not to bring any alcoholic beverages aboard ship.

American cigarettes were selling for $10 a carton and I had over twenty cartons stored in my sea bag. Taking advice from a merchant marine, I sneaked two cartons off the ship each liberty day by sticking them in my socks. I also filled my pockets with chocolate bars. I would sell the cigarettes to the more prosperous Belgians and the chocolate bars I handed to small children who would stare at me and be afraid to accept what I offered them. Some of the younger ones had never tasted a chocolate bar. The ones that took them would lick them like you would ice cream.

A few of us hunted around till we found a cellar bar with native beer. With nothing to eat, not even crackers, we tanked all the beer we could hold and started across the city to our ship. By the time we got there, the beer we had drunk had died out, leaving us hungry and dry. The only thing we had eaten since a light breakfast was one chocolate bar each. We raided the fridge that was kept stocked with all kinds of cold cuts and canned fruits, filling ourselves with fresh milk the purser had gotten from a food supplier, and with fresh lettuce, tomatoes, and green onions. We sat around in the mess hall for a while, listening to buzz rockets pass overhead. Every now and then, antiaircraft would explode one in its flight.

Each of us had to do an eight-hour watch twice during the next twenty-four hours at midnight. I sneaked off and hit the bunk for the next five hours. When I awoke I was restless. I had dreamed all night of home and the coal mines. I thought I was loading coal and the roof had started falling. I was pinned with big boulders of fallen rock and yelling for help. It seemed so real when I first awoke, until I got my senses as to where I was.

I dressed and reported for duty in the mess hall, where the coxswain ordered us to certain posts to stand guard. During our eight-hour shifts of guard, each man was relieved thirty minutes every two hours to relieve himself or to visit the fridge for a snack.

After a few more liberties I was learning my way around the city. I visited the one and only zoo I have ever seen. There were animals there that were hard to believe existed. The zoo was in back of a large railroad station. The station had designs built all through it. One figure I'll never forget was of a small boy holding his penis in his hand. Copies of this statue were seen in a lot of public places. Its history goes back several centuries to a young prince who got lost and this was the position he was found in.

Coming back to the States from Antwerp, the convoy didn't have as much escort as it did going over. Subs were working through the convoy. Two empty tankers were hit and the smoke could be seen from four ships five columns off the port side. Depth charges were dropped by fast-moving escort boats, and oil slicks could be seen forming on the surface. Fighter planes from the two flattops started circling the convoy, giving directions for changing course and telling where to drop depth charges.

During this sub attack a high wind moved in, bringing heavy rain. Visibility was zero and our electrical power went out. The captain ordered the engine room to idle the ship's engine and stop the propeller. The waves tossed the ship around like it was a toy. The rain kept coming in great torrents, blocking our vision. Without electrical power we were in danger of colliding with the other ships. The ship would pitch and roll several degrees. Nothing could be done to restore the power unit until the sea calmed down.

We rode the storm out. The winds moved off, but it was pitch black dark. Distress rockets were fired about every ten minutes until daylight. We must have wallowed in the sea for seven or eight hours. Just as soon as the ship stopped pitching and rolling, repair was started on the power unit.

When it got light enough to see, not a ship could be seen. During the sub attack and the storm all the columns had broken.

The ship was put in motion and a course was set. The power unit could not be repaired at sea. A hook-up was made from the main engine bypassing the blanked-out unit. Communication was being made to the admiral's ship and the formation of the convoy was put in position. We were told that eleven ships had been lost during the attack. Three hundred and fifty-seven survivors were picked up. Several planes had not made it back to the carriers.

The convoy, as usual, split up three days from the American shore. We anchored in the Hudson River, with the Statue of Liberty just off our port side. Fresh foods and mail were brought aboard. An ammunition boat came alongside and all the ammo we had aboard was lowered to its deck. At night all the food that had been put aboard before we left was dropped over the side. The purser didn't want to be caught with an oversupply of stock aboard. The issuers would cut him short next time if too much was brought back.

When all the ammo had been taken off, harbor tugs moved in to guide us to port. We tied up at a Norwegian berth. A new gun crew came aboard and took over. The entire crew I was in reported to the armed guard center. We presented our pay chits at the disbursement office and received our pay up to date. Then we were directed to the O.D.'s office to be handed a twenty-one day leave, with delayed orders for duty in the South Pacific.

Taking all our gear, each man started making schedules for home. I rode the famous Flamingo Special from New York's Grand Central to Bristol, Tennessee. From there to Harlan I rode mini-buses over the mountains. I arrived at home unannounced.

I entered the house from the back. The children were out front playing. Mae was doing a washing. I eased the door open and sneaked up near her. She turned and saw me standing there and nearly fainted. I hadn't called her to let her know I was back in the States.

After the shock, she called the children in and they took over, each one trying to outdo the other to get to me. With a lot of hugging and loving over, we got settled down to talking. I was trying to answer the questions, but they were coming too fast. They wanted to know if I had won the war and had come home to stay. I evaded some of the answers by promising to hurry and whip the Japs and then we could all be together again.

The twenty-one day leave was spent entirely with my family. The children made every step I did. We all enjoyed doing things together, romping and playing games. I built a tall post swing, with swing ropes twenty feet long and a strong seat to make them safe from falling out.

It was now time for me to leave. With a lot of good-byes and promises to hurry back, I left. When I arrived at Louisville I reported to a naval office, handing in my sealed orders. About 500 sailors were jam-packed in the basement, where we were informed of our transportation to the Pacific coast. We were given meal tickets for three meals a day, no price limit. The coaches were pullmans and each sailor had his own berth with privacy. Civilians rode the same coaches. This was far different from the other troop trains I had ridden in.

We lived in this luxury for seven days and nights. The train pulled into Oakland, California, and a fleet of navy buses took us to Shoemaker for special gunnery training. The bus ride took us on back roads to avoid the public and photographers. Our special training was to be hush-hush. We were forbidden to talk to other naval personnel about it. The back roads leading to Shoemaker went through beautiful country. Vineyards were all along the way. Large citrus groves covered many square miles, and some fields of over a thousand acres had nothing but lettuce.

This special training was for occupational duty on islands that had been recovered by the allies. We also had to learn a lot of mannerisms so we could cope with the natives and get all the information we could from them. The schooling lasted for thirty days. No liberty and no base duty to pull, just thirty days of listening to the different classes of survival teachings and the handling of special weapons.

Victory in Europe had come and something big had been planned for the Pacific fighting. These special trained groups were transferred to Treasure Island, California, to go aboard ships that would take us to the Hawaiian Islands.

The biggest decision that was ever made was when the president ordered an atomic bomb attack on Hiroshima. I was at sea then, three days from port. Scuttlebutt had it going that the atomic bomb had destroyed Hiroshima and that Japan had surrendered. All the armed forces were allowing discharges for personnel that had the required number of points. The point system was based on the length of service, where it was served, the number of dependents, your age, and the duties you had performed. In order to be discharged each man had to have at least 260. My points amounted to over 400.

The ships anchored offshore and all personnel were mustered on deck and told of the surrender of Japan. All the men wishing for discharge who had enough points could leave ship and billet in the Pearl Harbor area until passage could be made back to the States. Requisitions were filled and passage was made for me on the *Amsterdam*, a light cruiser just under the size of a big battleship. The regular crew was over 2,500. We who were coming back for separation centers numbered over 4,000.

Hammocks were hung anywhere on the decks you could find to stretch one. The eating lines were continued all day. When you finished eating breakfast, you lined up for dinner. The sides of the ship were used to urinate over more than the heads were used. Seasickness affected the moods of a lot of the men that had been stationed on the islands. Men that didn't have seasickness got to puking and gagging just from listening to the others heave and try to vomit.

A few poker games could be found throughout the ship, and dice games were everywhere a group could be formed. My luck was holding out pretty good in poker. My winnings amounted to over $200, which I soon lost shooting craps.

My sea bag, containing all my gear plus a few trinkets I had picked up at different ports for my wife and children, had been taken from a gun tub post that I had securely tied it to. The P.A. system announced a $50 reward for anyone reporting its whereabouts, but I never saw it again. Having made friends with several of the men, I soon had enough clothes to last me through the separation center.

The *Amsterdam* was met by river pilots and powerful tugs at the inlet of the Columbia River. With slowness and expert guidance at the wheel, the big ship made its way to Portland, Oregon, and tied up at the shipyards. It was the largest ship that had ever come up the Columbia. Thousands lined the banks, waving banners, and small planes kept circling the ship, trailing streamers with "Welcome Home" in big letters. Some places, where the river was narrow, school bands dressed in bright uniforms would be playing music. Every man aboard ship was on deck, receiving the welcome home tribute.

The processing office was understaffed and a lot of men were sent to other centers for discharge. I was sent to Great Lakes, Illinois. I soon had my discharge papers and was on my way home.

SEVENTEEN

WHILE RIDING a passenger train from Chicago to Harlan, I began thinking of the many ways to provide a better life for my family. I couldn't see going back to work in the coal mines for some big company and only earning enough to get by on. I was a fairly good trader in livestock and I had my license to operate a mine of my own if I could muster up enough money to set one up. The demand for coal was just as great now as it had been through the war. All this was running through my brain as the train pulled into the Harlan depot.

"Welcome Home" banners were stretched across the main streets of town, and victory hats were worn by the people that ran the town and also by those that had been deferred, namely, 4-F'ers. My family was there, along with my wife's brother, to greet me. Hundreds of parents and wives were there to greet their sons and husbands.

The place my wife had moved to from Benham coal camp was on the edge of the town of Harlan. The houses were jam-packed, allowing very little front, with a small garden in the back. I wanted something better. My five children needed more area than this provided. On my second day at home I went to Cumberland, Kentucky, and leased a better home with a lot of land. Moving my family to this new surrounding gave them a whole new look on life. A small grade school was near and a good stream of mountain water flowed at the back of the property. A big pasture faced the front, with knee-high grass all over it. We just turned the children loose and watched them enjoy themselves with the freedom given them.

It being several miles from here to Benham, I decided I would go back to work for the company long enough to claim bonuses and vacation pay that was due me. I worked one month to become eligible to receive the money due me.

In the meantime, I had bought us a good Chevrolet car and a fine riding horse. On weekends, when visiting the town of Cumberland, I started inquiring about coal land to lease. Several small holdings were available, but I wanted a large acreage.

The superintendent of the Wise County, Virginia, schools owned thousands of acres in Kentucky, with several seams of fine quality coal on it, at the head of the Cumberland River. A good blacktop road fronted it, giving good access to a railhead by truck. I visited Mr. Kelly, the owner, at his office. After a few pleasantries, we got down to discussing my leasing the property he owned in Kentucky. A nominal royalty per ton as mined was agreed on and all his holding of mineral was leased to me for ten cents per ton as it was mined.

The frontage along the contour of the mountain had been strip-mined and the seams left exposed for several miles. A good graded road had been built for trucking the stripmined coal to the blacktop highway. I had enough money to set up a quick way to get coal to the railhead at Cumberland. I bought three rubber-tired wheel-barrows and enough lumber to build ramps to wheelbarrow the coal after it was blasted loose up into the waiting trucks.

I employed ten to fifteen men, some drilling and blasting, others rolling wheelbarrows loaded with a good quality of coal. Money was coming my way. I soon financed the cost of building a large tipple and equipping a working condition underground, using small working ponies to haul low-tonnage cars of coal to the surface.

The following winter, with the increase of small truck mines and automation of the big mines, the supply yards of all the consumers were overstocked and the price of coal dropped. The smaller mines like my own couldn't compete with mechanical mines, and a lot of us went broke.

My fifth son, Shade, was born about this time and I kept plugging away, trying to keep my mines operating, sometimes by myself, to keep payments up on the indebtness incurred during my try at competing with the larger mines.

My struggle to hold onto my lease and mining equipment was proving useless. I owned no property to put up for collateral and the banks wouldn't talk to me about a loan. Nick Lawrence owned the coal tipple at the railhead and stopped buying truck-mined coal. He owned three truck mines himself. Trucking his own coal and running it through his own tipple, he managed to sell enough at the low price to stay in business.

The lease and the equipment I had put together were a promising investment if I could last through the slump in the coal sales. I talked to Nick about him taking over my indebtedness for the mines and paying me for the hand tools and ponies that were free of debt. The lease and all the other mining equipment could be transferred to him and his company. This was agreed on. I was paid for all the privately owned material I had accumulated while operating the mines.

I could have gone back to work at Benham, but pride kept me from doing so. I had been a failure operating my own mine and thought I might be ridiculed by the men I had worked with. I had to get work soon. Another baby was on the way.

I got a job at Lynch, Kentucky, loading coal and operating a locomotive when I was needed. This was the largest coal mine in the state. Their daily tonnage was 5,000 tons, their work force around 1,500.

Our last baby was born while I was working at this mine. I hadn't accumulated much wealth during our marriage, but I was a millionaire in babies. So Mae and I decided we were rich enough and this one would be the last one.

Carolyn was born demanding from the start. She would have nothing to do with taking seventh place sucking the breast. She had to have several different brands of the most expensive baby food and milk. She has a family of her own now, and she is yet as demanding and positive as she was when she was a baby.

Since working at the Lynch coal mine had given me knowledge of blasting underground, I was asked to direct the drilling and blasting of a huge tunnel connecting one seam of coal up through two thousand foot of solid sandstone to another seam. This was a dangerous job. The height of the tunnel made it difficult to detect loose rock. Great boulders and shattered spots would fall loose all during the working hours. Very seldom would it fall during the idle hours. It was decided that the forced air going in during the working hours created pressure in the cracks and caused it to fall. But with careful workers and caution signs posted, no serious accidents happened, from start to finish of the job.

The Lynch Coal Company refused to hire me back in the mines. My background had reached them and while they were shed of me they didn't want any organizer in their employ. I tried at other mines for work but got the same denial from them. I was being blackballed all over Harlan County. My funds were about all gone and Mae and I discussed what to do. I knew it would be useless to keep going

163

from mine to mine, seeking work. The Blue Diamond Coal Company I had first worked for was getting back at me for the union organizing I had done while working for them.

All seven of our children, including Carolyn, the baby, were sitting at the supper table, the older ones suggesting we move to another county to live. Letcher County was decided on. It was a coal mining county and I was not known there for my union activities. It was the county my wife was from. She's from a large clan named Combs that had migrated from England. Some of them are very prominent in various businesses. Mae's father, Shade Combs, was a career schoolteacher, having taught forty-seven years all over the county. The more successful men throughout Letcher County give credit to his strict teaching for their knowledge in conducting many forms of business.

The next day I went over the mountains to Whitesburg and learned that a lot of the smaller mines were in need of management. I let it be known that I was a certified mining and first aid supervisor with license to operate and manage any number of miners in the state of Kentucky. I was soon swamped with offers from several owners. It was my decision to hire with Willis B. Banks, a well known man of honesty and very wealthy. He owned four truck mines and was barely running enough tonnage to meet his payroll. He went with me to visit each mine, introducing me to the foremen, telling them that I was the manager and had complete charge of the operation of all four of his mines. I was furnished a four-wheel drive jeep to travel from one mine to the other, making friends with all the employees and foremen.

One morning each week all the miners at one mine would willingly attend a production and safety meeting. Films were shown of different methods of mining coal and how to avoid the dangers of unsafe conditions caused by mismanagement. Workers at these mines got to liking the way their tonnage and safety programs were progressing and looked forward each week to another film.

All the coal loaders were being paid for the number of cars and the amount per car. Some of the men worked in disadvantaged places, such as with bad roof conditions, or lower-level places with water two to six inches deep. I changed this per car pay and put each man that worked in these places on an hourly pay equal to what the other hourly men were earning. This pleased everyone, including Wid Banks.

Still, my job with the Banks Coal Company showed nothing but a weekly paycheck. The expenses of raising seven children and keeping them dressed halfway decent for school kept Mae busy stretching the paycheck week after week, to have a balanced diet, to keep them healthy and happy. I thought if I could lease a mine from someone I could earn a better living for them. Several small mines were idle, due to not having certified management. I could take my choice from any of them.

I selected one from a long list of closed mines. Claud Collins was the owner. During the growth of truck mining, Claud had purchased a fleet of Diamond T. Trucks, contracting them to haul coal from many different mines to the railhead. The mines I leased from him had been a losing venture for him. He had lost money each week he operated them because of the lack of management.

It took me about two weeks to change over from using ponies and mining cars on steel rails to a new method of getting coal from far underground. By using an electric drag cable coal buggy, hauling two to four tons at each load, my weekly pay was about double what I'd been making using just one buggy.

Claud decided to sell me the mines. He was going into politics and didn't want to be bothered with them. The amount I was to pay was agreed on and weekly payments were to be made, giving me an opportunity to build more rubber-tired coal buggies.

My sons were of great help during their out-of-school days. Some would carry supplies up the mountain, while others kept the rock picked out of the coal as it was dumped in the tipple. This was a family-operated mine. My wife did the bookkeeping. My expenses were low due to the help my boys were giving me.

The lease I was working was what is termed a pillar mine. All the advance work having been done, the supporting blocks of coal along the haulways would be blasted and hauled to the tipple, allowing the mountain to cave in when several of these supporting blocks were removed. This kind of mining was very dangerous.

It took me about two years to remove the blocks of coal from the main depth all the way to the drift mouth. During this time we bought us a small house, which we soon enlarged into a very comfortable home. I was now the proud father of seven children, all going to the same school at the same time. They went to the Whitesburg School. Only one other man had bested me. Big John Brown has taken over the record by having twelve children going to the same school at the same time. But, as I said, his name was "Big John" Brown.

Having gotten all minable coal from this mine and paid Claud for the equipment, I started looking around for another idle mine to lease. Most all the idle ones had been shut down because of a faulty roof or too much water seeping in. Some had had all the advance work done, leaving large blocks supporting the haulways. The owners, not having experience in pillar mining, would cease work and open another mine nearby.

Using the equipment I had bought from Claud, I leased and worked out several pillar mines throughout the county, always earning more money doing this than I would have made managing a mine for someone else.

My children were getting grown by now. The second one, Norma, had married and lived in Louisville. Bill, the oldest, was in college at Pippa Passes, Kentucky. Buck, the third child, had grown to a large man and decided he wanted to become a barber. He was enrolled in barber school at Louisville. The other four children were enjoying their high school years.

Bill married a neighbor girl and quit college. He soon volunteered for army duty and went to Germany. His wife joined him there. While stationed in Germany he finished several college courses and in the meanwhile a son was born to them. This made me a grandpa for the second time, Norma beating him by three years to become the mother of a son.

My next two sons, after completing high school at the same time, decided they wanted to see some of the world. They joined the army. Benny, my fourth child, was sent to Korea and learned to operate heavy equipment. Dave was in the engineering department and was sent to Germany. My family was decreasing every year. Shade, my fifth child, was graduating from high school and had been accepted at Morehead State University.

New highways were replacing the dangerous narrow trails and gravel roads throughout the mountains of Eastern Kentucky, blasting the mountains down to near the level of the valleys. One long stretch of Highway 15 was under construction coming into Whitesburg. I decided I'd had enough coal mining, and hired on with the drilling and blasting crew on this stretch of road. I was soon put in charge of the surface blasting of the largest mountain that had ever been moved for the construction of a road. From the top of the mountain to the road level, measured straight down, was 368 feet.

My skill at keeping the blasting expenses low soon spread to other contractors and I was being offered more pay to work for them. I took the better offers and continued at this kind of work until all the nearby highways were completed.

The last job of my road-building career was on a bypass of Kingsport, Tennessee, having been called there to do difficult blasting near the city's residential area, leaving Mae and Carolyn home. Carolyn was in her last year of school. Shade was off in college. The others, five of them married, were scattered from Louisville to Florida.

Kingsport being too far away to travel daily to work, I was batching near the job and coming home only on weekends. A good friend of mine, one of the most powerful politicians in Letcher County, met me on the street on one of my weekends. I had laid off from work to travel through the rugged part of the county getting voters to elect him to office. He told me he could offer me a good government job if I had a high school diploma. I told him my schooling had been limited under hardships and the fourth grade was as high as I ever got. He insisted I take a test for an equivalent certificate at Pikeville College. I told my wife about this. Shade, coming home from college each weekend, started tutoring me on the most likely subjects that would be listed in the test.

On the third weekend after the offer, I took the test and passed the required grade. When I received my certificate, I presented it to my politician friend. The job he had offered me required me to stay away from home more than half the time, at my own expense, and I was to furnish my own transportation throughout three adjoining counties, setting up work programs for the state's elderly citizens' aid society. After spending a whole day going over the planning of the programs, and purchasing a car to travel in, I asked how often I would be reimbursed for my expenses.

He said, "This is an honorly job. The only pay you will get would be a very low monthly salary."

I asked him what the hell was my family to live on while I was doing this. His answer was that he could help my wife draw food relief through the welfare office.

I told him, "I think this is the damnedest job offer I have ever heard of," and he could shove it up his ass and all the other politicians' asses. I stormed out of his office. He had been the county court clerk for the past five four-year terms and is now on his eighth term. The famous quote from Benjamin Franklin was, "You can fool part of the people all the time, but you can't fool all the people all of the time." This man was doing the reverse. He had fooled the people of this county for the past half century and is a master at doing it yet. With the training he has given some of his family, they will hold the political power for years to come.

My blasting and drilling job finished in 1969, and with nothing to do I planned on a restful winter until another road job would demand my services in the spring. As I came into the house a few days before Thanksgiving, carrying a load of my batching gear I had been using in Kingsport, Mae was talking on the phone to our son Benny in Naples, Florida. She handed me the phone and said, "Here's Benny. He wants to talk to you."

Benny started off telling me what a nice day it had been. He planned to go fishing that night. The main reason he called was he wanted me to come there for the winter. There was plenty of work going on and I could pick my job from many different construction sites.

I told him I had just finished my job in Tennessee and thought I might come. "First I'd better talk it over with your Mom."

We talked on for a while, him telling me I was missing out being around the most of my grandchildren. Dave living near, we got to see his two boys often, but like Benny said, the others were growing up as strangers to me.

I sorta wanted to get out of the cold weather. Mae started nodding her head for me to agree to come down. I told him we had agreed with a head nod, and to expect me in a few days.

The next day Mae started picking out and sorting my clothes. She was to stay there until I located a house and a job. Benny was two jumps ahead of me on these. He had spoken to his superintendent about me coming to Naples to work and live. He told Benny not to inquire any further. He was sure he could use me at one of the many openings on Marco Island.

EIGHTEEN

I FLEW FROM Lexington to Atlanta, then on to Miami. I was seated midway at a window on a night flight. It was a clear night, no clouds anywhere, as the plane neared Atlanta. It started circling the city for landing. I thought I had seen some big cities, but looking at Atlanta from above at night, and it clear of clouds and smog—it's something I'll never forget. The lights appeared like needlework, patterned from someone's idea of an emerald, glittering with thousands and thousands of diamonds. If I could take a paintbrush and a large canvas and transfer the picture of this that is in my head for you to see, you would have to agree it's a beautiful scene to remember. But me not knowing which end of a brush to use, you will have to accept the description I have tried to give you.

Bill and Buck met me at Miami and we drove to Naples. I spent my first night at Bill's. The next day being a Sunday, Bill wanted me to go fishing out in the Gulf with him and a friend of his, Dale Cain. I was the only one fishing. Bill and Dale just wanted to talk business. We moved to the inland waters and I caught a few catfish. Bill and Dale came to some kind of an agreement on their talk and we came back in to the dock.

The evening was still early and I got with Benny and Buck. They drove me to the house that Benny lived in. It was a small two-bedroom, partly furnished. He was moving in with his widowed mother-in-law to care for her. He wanted me to take over his indebtedness on the house. I had expected it and had brought my clothes from Bill's. I always thought it best to try to not be a bother to my kin. I knew I would be welcome and treated kindly at their home, but my aim was to get settled and make Florida my home.

The next morning Benny came by to pick me up. I had done some grocery shopping the evening before. Me being an early riser, I had fixed a good mountain breakfast—fried salt bacon, potatoes, eggs, milk gravy, and a pan of light fluffy biscuits. Benny said, "I'm running late for work, but I'm sure not going to pass up a breakfast like this, even if I lose my job."

I had batched and camped on wagon trains most of my life and knew how to make any kind of food come to its full flavor. After Benny gorged himself with the first mountain breakfast he had eaten since he had come to Florida, we took off to Marco Island, where he worked for a large development company.

I met Benny's superintendent and was shown around the island and shown some of the work that was being done. Huge drag lines were digging canals through mangrove swamps, piling dug-up sand and shells ahead to level off the land for them to move ahead on. The drag line would settle itself on the built-up sand and shells and move on ahead again.

The operator would start digging and piling sand and shells forty to fifty feet high into the mangrove swamps. After the piles had drained, big dozers would smooth them down to level over the swamps. Sea wall crews would follow, jetting down huge concrete slabs to become a beautiful wall to check the sand from feeding back into the canal. Later, streets and nice homes would be built.

People were coming from all over the world, mostly people from the northern parts of the United States who were retired and looking for a place in the sun to enjoy boating and fishing and a lazy way to live out their remaining years. They'd be shown the beautiful homes with open canals to the Gulf. Palm trees, grass, and flowery shrubbery would decorate the lawns and medians of the streets. Boat docks would be installed for each home. Back-door fishing or basking in the sun could be seen at nearly every home.

After the superintendent took me over the parts of the island under his supervision, he asked me if I was ready to begin work any time this week. A night shift was due to start that night and I could start oiling on one of the larger drag lines, day or night shift. I asked for the night shift. I wanted to do a lot of work around the tiny house I had taken over so as to accommodate my grandchildren and their moms and dads.

It was about thirty miles from Naples to Marco Island. Bill had a Volkswagen and lent it to me to drive to and from work. I started work that next night.

I had called Mae and told of buying the house Benny had lived in, and that I was having it refurnished. I told her how beautiful

Naples and Marco Island were and that the weather was just like summertime. I told her to lock the house and fly on down, she would love it.

My three daughters-in-law tried to outdo each other in helping me clean, paint, and refurnish the house. When Mae arrived, everything was in perfect order. She loved it and thought we should call it our honeymoon cottage. She went over it, changing the furniture around to suit herself.

One or two days a week, we would go to the beach and cook hamburgers or hotdogs. Some days the daughters-in-law would go with us. I had nothing to do during the day but lay around and sleep, and I could do that on a quilt down on the beach.

The night crew worked ten-hour shifts. The operator I was oiling for would come to work tanked up, with a bottle in his lunch pail. After a few nights he put me to swinging the drag bucket out and dragging it in empty. He would allow me to do this for an hour or two each night for about a week. Then he told me to start loading the bucket about half full and to increase the load slowly until I was sure of myself on the power and movements of the machine.

In about two weeks, I was doing the operating and he would pile up near the engine room with his bottle and go to sleep. The night foreman would make his rounds to this machine around lunch time. When I would see his lights bouncing around, coming our way, I would go back and rouse the operator. He would dash cold water to his face to wake himself and crawl into the cab and start digging. This was the way we worked until he and I were changed to the day shift. More people moved over the jobs during the day, so he slacked off on his drinking, but he let me do more digging than I did on the night shift.

The foreman would drive his Bronco up to where he could watch me operate, sometimes coming aboard and standing on the catwalk and watching the precision movements I was making. This machine was the largest on the island, using a six-yard bucket. Each bucketful, curled all the way to the spreader bar, would be the size of a pickup truck.

Not bragging, but I sure enjoyed curling them big buckets and swinging them out over the mangroves on this Monday morning. I had the machine greased and the engine room spotless. The big Cummings diesel was wiped clean and idling smoothly, but my operator hadn't showed up by about nine o'clock. I raised the boom and hoisted the bucket. That was the way to let yourself be known of a breakdown, or that you needed the foreman. My signal was spotted and the foreman drove up.

I told him that A.D., the operator, had failed to come to work. He asked me if I wanted to be the operator. I said, "That's fine with me." He told me to sit tight till he got me an oiler. You don't operate a machine that big without an oiler to keep check on oil or fuel leaks and continuously wipe the motor and to assist with minor breakdowns.

I worked in some of the more difficult swamps. This area was being rushed so as to meet a digging permit from the Army Corps of Engineers. It was decided to put the digging on two twelve-hour shifts. I asked to go back on the night shift. It was getting hot during these summer months, and the nights were a lot cooler.

These twelve-hour shifts continued for ninety days, seven days a week. Benny had been put in charge of night shift crews and was getting more yardage than the day shift with the same machines.

Me and a few of the closer operators decided on having a barbecue on Fridays, each one bringing steaks or ribs and some bringing drinks, bread, and baked beans. I brought dutch style potatoes and did the cooking.

My oiler had learned to operate the rig as good as I could. At the beginning of the Friday night shift all the food would be transferred to me. I'd place all the meat in a large cooler. About two hours before our mid-shift, I'd build a big fire of buttonwood and lay a large square of meshed catwalk metal over it and start preparing our food, sometimes fixing twenty pounds of steak and fifty pounds of ribs. Setting the pots and pans of beans and potatoes near the heat on a half sheet of plyboard, I'd season the meat and start it cooking. I made the sauce at home. We would use over a gallon. Every time we cooked, the aroma could be smelled for miles all over the island.

The day shift soon learned of our Friday night doings and reported it to the superintendent. He started making rounds during the nights. When Friday came, we went ahead with our plans to have our barbecue. All the drag lines were operating smoothly. I built a big fire and started cooking. I noticed headlights on a vehicle a short distance away blink out. At a few minutes past midnight, the crews that were going to eat started driving up. I had all the meat cooked and simmering in sauce. The baked beans and baked potatoes were hot.

Everybody lined up and helped themselves. Plenty of food was left. Whoever had pulled up and turned the headlights off was still there. Someone went towards where the car was parked and called out, "Come and have something to eat!"

The answer was, "I didn't think you was ever going to ask me." The superintendent walked up and said, "The aroma from that cooking was starving me!" I told him to grab a plate and dig in.

There were sixteen of us, not including Benny and the superintendent. As the men finished their eating they would go back to their rigs and be ready to start digging at one o'clock. The superintendent enjoyed about six or eight ribs and all the other food he wanted. He said he didn't see a damn thing wrong with us having a good barbecue on Friday nights or any other night we wanted to, but to look for him to come up around eating time.

The end of the digging permit time was drawing near and some of the rigs that had completed their assigned stretches of canal were rushed to other canals that were behind in their digging. On the last day's digging on this permit, we were three days ahead of schedule.

These ninety-some days, twelve hours a day, with no days off, made the whole crew snappy and irritable at each other. Some of the rig crews were laid off. I was put back on the day shift, filling in on any machine that was without an operator. I welcomed it, as I hadn't gotten to be with the boys' families for the past three months.

Mae was doing poorly. She kept having chest pains. Her doctor would change her medicine nearly every week. He finally had her to see a heart specialist and she was sent to Miami Heart Institute to have bypasses to her heart. I sure thought I was losing her.

I went in to see her in the recovery room. I looked at her with all the tubes and monitors on her and I started one of my silent prayers for her to get well and not leave me. I got to thinking what a miserable life it would be without her. I never was much to make over affections, but if the Lord would let her live, I promised to be more considerate of her.

That has been five years ago. Mae recovered rapidly but has to continue taking medicine daily and visit her doctor regularly. I've retired from work and have the enjoyment of being able to stay at home to be with her.

It looks like our fate is to spend our remaining years here in Florida. We let our son Dave, our fifth child and fourth son, have the home we left in Kentucky. With plenty of time on our hands and Mae's fast recovery, we decided we'd like to have a place, maybe just a shack, back there among the mountains to go to in the summers and be with Dave's family and the many friends we left there.

We loaded our pickup with what building tools we had and headed for the hills with a small camper behind us. It was early spring and the mountains were in full bloom with beautiful dogwood, redbud, sarvis, and many other early budding trees. Our son Bill had bought a large tract of land away from the town, about six miles out, in a remote area, and wanted us to build a cabin on it. With the help of friends I soon had it built. It's not large but it's mighty comfortable.

Every summer we raise us some hogs to butcher in the fall and cure the meat with sugar curing salt. The cool days and cold nights bring out the desired flavor. We also do a lot of canning of fruits and wild berries. At Sunday morning breakfasts it's exciting to watch our children and grandchildren enjoy the good mountain food we bring back to Florida.

I've tried unsuccessfully to get Dave to give up coal mining and come on down. That sounds good, just like the TV show "The Price Is Right." But he wants to stay up there in Kentucky and be near his two sons since his divorce. Dave has married again to a wonderful girl, and she has borne him a fine baby girl. He's much happier on his second time around. He stays in close togetherness with his two sons and sees to their welfare and health.

I've tried to do a little cattle raising here in Florida but it failed. Now I look forward to going on wagon train trips over the rugged mountains of North Carolina. I've made two trips and come back feeling years younger.

With a lot of time between wagon train trips, I got to thinking about my past and thought I'd like to try my hand at writing about it. If you've read this book and enjoyed the way I've told of the life I've lived and the experiences I've had with violence and love and tragedies, you know it's not all a very pretty picture to tell. But I've done the best I can to explain it. I'm about finished with this writing and some of my friends want me to write about the wagon train trips I've made. I might just do it when I come back from visiting Harlan.

EPILOGUE

I GO BACK to Harlan every year or so. I drive through the mountains and the memories of the past come back—the close calls I've had with violence, the many times I've witnessed beatings by hired thugs who would just as soon kill their victim as to beat him. I park along the now-paved roads and shudder when I look over the tops of the mountains and think of the times I nearly froze on them. I remember traveling these hills and mountains with large groups of wagons, never dreaming that those rutted and rugged roads would change into broad paved highways.

Like the old saying goes, time changes everything. Harlan is now a beautiful mountain town. A lot of people have prospered from the vast seams of coal that have been mined, in spite of having seen their share of violence. Where shanties once stood, homes that now stand in the same place look like mansions.

Some of the old mining shanties are still standing, but they look like they're about ready to collapse. I remember how in the beginning of building them, miners fought with each other for the right to move into them.

When I drive up the winding paved road that has been blasted from the mountain, I can find the farm I once called home. The big fields I plowed to raise corn and other foods in have been blocked off into building lots. Big fine trailer homes and frame houses reach from the foot of the mountain to the head of it. The last piece of new ground that I helped clear with my team of big black mules now has a nice two-story brick home on it. A big red barn is near the spring I used to drink from. A white board fence encloses about five acres. A white gravel driveway circles the big green lawn. I've sat and looked at the changes that have been made since the last time I was told to leave, and wondered what it might have been like if I'd belonged here from my beginning.

I always think of my sister Artie when I let my mind drift back. I think about the times she mothered me with love and care when I'd be feverish with a cold or when I was shunned by my mother and the others. But she's gone now, bless her. She didn't suffer much, till the last few breaths. She still loved Amos in her last words, although she'd been divorced from him for several years. Her last words were to our sister Narciss, to tell her to be sure supper would be ready when Amos came in from work. Then she stopped breathing.

I've seen Amos over the years since they parted. He was a preacher and toured in the early morning hours to a radio station in the little town of Cumberland to broadcast his sermons. He preached against having the town vote wet. The closeness with one of his singers that toured with him brought a fondness that turned to love, so she divorced her coal-mining husband and Amos divorced Artie. They were soon married and she bore him a fine son.

Artie never bore Amos a child, but they adopted a baby girl we all loved. She died in a car wreck. Artie later married a fine gentleman some years her senior. She lost him three years before her own death.

During Artie's last illness, a sister of ours denounced her kin to me in the presence of the hospital staff. I'd tried to live down my heritage by never saying anything about it to anyone, not even Mae. But I think, and always will, that Dad and one of my brothers-in-law, by the name of York, have told her many times. York started asking questions. Why was I so different from all the rest? One night, when he and Dad were getting drunk on moonshine, Dad told him I was a woods colt. A woods colt is a person that doesn't know who his father is. He said he didn't want me around him and his children.

My sister Artie has told me many times of the facts of my heritage. I was born in Eagan, Tennessee, from a whirlwind courtship in 1913. I was then taken to Harlan County the same month I was born. My mother's husband, the man I learned to call Dad, accepted my mother back and later came to hate me. Artie had the same father as I did.

My mother, in her last years, was mostly unloved by the other children and came to live with me and my wife till she passed away. Her husband had preceded her about ten years before that.

When I think about my mother, I think too about Mrs. Walters and her kindnesses to me. She never made a difference between me and her own. I went to see her often before her passing in 1939. I loved her dearly and wept openly at her death.

JoJo left the mountains to travel around the country. He could always make a hand at anything he wanted to do. He never had any education either, but he did real good work at any laboring or roustabout work he did. The last I heard of him was at Mrs. Walters' funeral. A lot of people have said some bad things about him, but he'd always been a very special friend of mine and I don't believe any of them stories are true.

The big thick seams of coal that brought wealth to these hills have been mined out. Only the scars left on the mountains remain, where the drifts were made. They're not the only scars left. Many a widowed wife remains with a torn and broken heart that's had to kneel before the big powerful coal lords and the elected criminals that brought the destruction of entire families to these mountains. I've heard of many violent deaths that were met from the imported thugs. Some of the biggest mine operators supposedly committed suicide, but I'll never believe they inflicted a hurt to themselves.

I guess I'm one of the lucky ones. I've seen it all happen but I'm still alive and so are my family. I've wondered many times if the good things that happened to me in my later years were brought about to repay me for the bitter years of my growing up. The love and closeness of my wife and children and grandchildren have brought me a happiness I can't describe in writing. Some people count their wealth in dollars. I count the health, happiness, and love we have for each other in the millions.

I think about the others, too, when I drive through those Kentucky mountains and look at the old places where so many things happened in my life. My brother Jim died with a bad heart. My youngest brother, Dave, worked in construction and was killed by a dozer accident. My brother William has lost his vision, but I stay in contact with him regularly. Narciss and Sophia died several years back. William and Cecil and I are all that remain of us.

I look back and remember and I feel bad for all the bloodshed and pain and suffering we knew. But then I go home again and look at what came out of it all. The house is full all the time with the children and grandkids that come visiting us. And I can look across the room at Mae and think again that I'm one of the lucky ones.